DEBUNKING
The
HYPERINFLATION
Of Peter Schiff And The Gold Bugs

DEBUNKING

The

HYPERINFLATION

Of Peter Schiff And The Gold Bugs

RICHARD MOHEBAN

MILE SANDS PRESS

Milwaukee, Wisconsin

TABLE OF CONTENTS

Introduction

In recent years, Euro Pacific Capital president Peter Schiff has become a guest of choice on various market news and economic talk show programs to present his contrasting and dire view of the US economy, what measures are now needed (no government assistance with any of the mortgage or corporate crises according to Schiff), and where we are headed next. He has surprised audiences and other pundit guests with his insistence that there is no near-term hope for the US economy and that regardless of what is done, we will soon certainly suffer a worst-case scenario of massive collapse of our economy that includes a severe spiral of devaluation of the US dollar (hyperinflation). He predicts US household wealth will bear much more financial suffering in addition to what has already been lost in the fallen real estate and stock markets. What makes his predictions especially frightening is that his was a lone voice in the financial media arena before 2007 who correctly predicted the housing bubble deflate, and the consequent subprime mortgage crisis. He was right in predicting that those events would send shock waves through the economy and cause additional crisis and recession, at a time when virtually no other pundits foresaw a serious downturn.

Mr. Schiff's doomsday scenario of far-worse-is-yet-to-come and his certainty of conviction motivated me to examine and research his conclusions and form my own. I am glad to say that after close investigation, research and original thought, I have found that the hyperinflation 'Armageddon' scenario purported by Schiff and other gold bugs is not only not a certainty, it is in fact a *very unlikely* result of the financial and economic crises facing the United States. Though our economy is contracting from the fallout of excessive debt levels and reeling under a still unknown extent of defaults to come, massive government stimulus being injected (financed with even more debt) need not necessarily result in double digit inflation, let alone hyperinflation. Assertions that they will are simply unfounded guesswork. Likely many more jobs will be lost in this crisis as employers tighten belts in response to falling revenues. The job loss will lead to lower consumer spending from the out-of-work, thus lower revenues, and more belt-tightening again. This self-feeding cycle may get quite ugly, but the specter of hyperinflation and the destruction of the US dollar are another matter. Let me explain.

CHAPTER ONE

The Schiff View and the Gold Bugs

Where Peter Schiff was spot-on was in his early prediction of the bursting of the housing price bubble and the consequent implosion of related debts. He understood how the housing market, in combination with the recent phenomenon of securitization of mortgages, had led to a new kind of frenzied home speculation without risking equity (little to nothing down). The downside risk was passed on through the lenders to the buyers of the mortgage-backed 'securities' (MBS), who were frequently our largest financial institutions or the central banks of foreign nations. In other words, he saw early on that home buyers who were traditionally unqualified were welcomed by lenders to speculate on the quickly rising home prices because these speculators risked little down payment, but would reap any appreciation. At the same time, many lenders cast off their traditional lending cautions because they quickly sold off the loans in so-called "diversified" mortgage backed securities (CMO's, REMIC's) to large institutional funds and foreign buyers. These subprime loan originators were taking lucrative origination fees as their primary incentive, so lacked the usual credit quality concerns as they sold off the loans. Meanwhile, the government (with its good intentions and poor oversight) was fueling this racket with historically low interest rates, programs to encourage homeownership, and mortgage guarantees for many. Often speculators, and legitimate homeowners, additionally had 'teaser' adjustable interest rates that would reset with much higher payments after a number of months, exacerbating defaults yet to come.

At the crux of the financial and credit market crisis of 2008-2009 was the uncertainty of the ultimate default levels to be experienced by the MBS holders, as well as other securitized consumer debts such as auto loans and credit card debts. Investors and depositors, having realized the tenuous nature of these supposedly safe 'diversified' securitized assets, fled from these securities and the stocks of the investment banks, deposit banks, and other major holders of these securities. The resultant exodus of money from these securities was so massive in 2008 that the supply overwhelmed the demand to the point that the market for these securitized products *ceased to function.* It is a critically different thing for a market of roughly equal buying and selling volume to reach equilibrium at a low price level (reflecting increased risk), than for selling volume to completely overwhelm demand volume in mass indiscriminate selling. When huge institutional sellers are forced to deleverage all at once with far fewer buyers around, the resulting prices have little bearing on the assets' fundamental value. Once these securities plunged in market value from mass selling, holders of all such similar securities were forced by relatively new "mark to market" accounting rules to write down their portfolios to the unrealistically depressed market values, causing massive realized paper losses and financial panic. In the case of mortgage-backed securities, the prices had fallen drastically in anticipation of mortgage default levels that had not, and still have not yet materialized![1] Unfortunately, mere appearances can become reality, and fire-sale priced securitized debt along with rapidly falling stock values have in turn created liquidity crises, insolvencies and bankruptcies, and launched the US and world into a serious recession.

Pivotal in causing the financial crisis was the relatively new "mark to market" accounting rules that forced holders of securitized debt to incur massive charges in writing down their asset portfolios to the meaningless market values created by mass deleveraging. The result of massive write downs in our major financial institutions' assets was panic gripping the financial markets and consequently, the economy, unfortunately before actual default levels proved to be particularly dire. There will be some self-fulfilling prophecy effect, as the ultimate severity of the recession affects the debtors' ability to pay, as does the stabilization point for home values. *Absolutely nobody* knows how bad defaults will ultimately be. It is a waiting game. The good news is that it seems a worst-case scenario has been priced into the markets, and anything less could ultimately be a real boon.

For the intelligent who were aware of these subprime

---

1   The most recent data released as of January 2009 of the percentage of total US bank loans in delinquency is 3.6%. Compared with a chronic 4%-6% rate between 1984 and 1994, these numbers suggest the default concerns may be overblown. Source: Wells Capital Management, 2008-Issue 7 & http://www.federalreserve.gov/releases/ChargeOff/delallnsa.htm

mortgage lending practices, it was not hard to see that this was going to end badly should home appreciation falter. Of course, home values cannot shoot up forever, and falter they did. But from here, Mr. Schiff goes on from the fairly easy analysis that a real estate bubble existed, to generalize and speculate with the direst of predictions for the US economy in general, and the US dollar. *It is important to note that there is a huge difference between recognizing a bubble in a specific asset class, and having investigated the nature of the speculation, discovering a racket and no fundamental justification for such prices, to predicting with any certainty major (and quite extreme) outcomes in a highly complex economy.* This is especially true when such extraordinary predictions require completely earth-shaking changes in perceptions of value (and risk) by tens of millions of economic participants across the globe.

It is interesting, and telling I believe, that Schiff presents his cause-and-effect predictions not as arguments backed up by any detailed, supportive, quantitative discussion, but by stating sweeping generalizations that are at times quite shocking and unusual, as simply facts. Conclusions that might require an entire dissertation to try to argue persuasively, he simply states as premises. He then quickly moves on to describe in detail his horrific scenario of which we are on the eve in this country. Shock and fear then replace clear-minded judgment for the listener. It is understandable in public media 'sound bites' to be brief, but his book, *Crash Proof: How to Profit from the*

Coming Economic Collapse, also disappoints in the search for detailed, quantitative support for his dire and certain predictions.

Paraphrasing from his media appearances and writings, the Schiff thesis would seem to go something like this:

> The US economy has become a largely "phony" economy because we have lost our productive (manufacturing) base. We are no longer a wealth-producing, exporting nation since we don't produce many physical goods in factories, but instead we are something of a freeloader nation to the rest of the world. Foreign capital is now financing our homes, credit card debt, and reckless consumer overconsumption, through securitization and then selling of our debts abroad. The US government and US dollar are being propped up by other countries, too, by way of large foreign investment in US Treasuries to fund massive deficit spending.[2] Both the US government and consumers are broke, with debts exceeding assets once overpriced US real estate and financial asset values plummet.

> Schiff discounts jobs in the service sector as unproductive and creating of no true national wealth. He asserts that the foreigners who now finance our private and public debt will cease financing new loans soon as they realize much of our debts are bad. Foreigners will also be burned holding bonds denominated in US dollars because the

---

2 Through the recent phenomenon of 'securitization', a large quantity of US consumer and mortgage debt has been packaged and sold, as has US Treasury debt, to foreign central banks and foreign investors. Much of this foreign demand stems from excess US dollars in foreign hands due to their trade surplus with the US.

dollar is sure to rapidly decline in massive inflation as well, leaving them with plummeting values in all their US assets. He has made the bold prediction that a best case scenario is the US dollar losing only half of its value in the very near future. He suggests, based on the recent massive Federal stimulus' borrowing and spending, the more likely scenario is the dollar going bust by losing at least 90% of its current value, perhaps much more.[3]

The foreign creditors to the US, having been burned by both defaults and the fallen dollar, will no longer want US paper at any price. US consumers thus won't be able to borrow and spend, but rather will be forced to live within their means and save. Since the US economy is driven (about two thirds) by consumer spending, a severe US Depression will follow. The US will not be able to recover wealth by selling goods abroad because we have little physical goods to export. The "phony" US economy (GDP) will deflate in value to nearer its actual physical production level, and require rebuilding of productive capacity (factories) by saving and investing in plant and equipment instead of the current "phony" economy driven by government stimulus and consumer spending. Pivotal to the Schiff hyperinflation thesis is the fatal flaw of our fiat currency[4], leading

---

3   There is little argument that such hyperinflation would be profoundly destructive to our economy and would drastically change our daily lives, so this bears investigation. A silver lining to moderately high inflation would be the boon for debtors, the biggest being of course the US Treasury. After high inflation occurs, one can pay off debts, which are in nominal dollars, quite cheaply with the inflated currency. The poor creditors receive only a pittance in real terms. In this sense, high inflation aids the encumbered out of the holes they have dug, and thus provides some general relief to any economic turmoil that includes moderate inflation. *Deflation* would have the opposite effect of digging the indebted down deeper, which is one reason the government prefers inflationary policies to deflation.

4   All nations today use fiat currency, meaning that their circulating money has no intrinsic

to massive loss of value of the US dollar (hyperinflation) through unchecked Federal Reserve money supply expansion in desperate attempt to stimulate the economy and service the national debt.

Distilling from my above representation of Schiff's thesis, the following are what I see as some of his implicit assumptions I will examine in subsequent chapters. Namely, that:

1) Consumption adds no value to the economy as it produces nothing.

2) Manufacturing creates national wealth while the service sector does not. The US has little manufacturing base anymore.

3) We are a bankrupt nation; our debts exceed our assets and earnings. Our paper wealth (real estate values as well as US-based securities) is phony and will largely evaporate as the crisis deepens and the US dollar plummets.

<u>*4) The unprecedented level of government borrowing*</u>

value or redeemability in any hard asset, such as gold. As recently as the 1960's many nations including the United States had money that was backed by silver or gold. Circulating US dimes, quarters and half dollars were made of 90% silver until 1965. Currency could be redeemed to the government at any time in exchange for bullion. Those days are gone for all nations today. This has led the "gold bugs" to sound the alarm that such fiat currencies are destined to suffer massive hyperinflative failure. They say that lacking the discipline of only printing paper money that is sufficiently covered by government bullion reserves, governments will eventually create far too much currency, causing rampant inflation and thereby the destruction of the fiat currency. When economies are troubled, gold bugs assert that politicians will attempt the popular antidote of stimulative spending and tax reductions, fueled by borrowing, and thus plant the hyperinflationary seeds of fiat currency destruction.

9

must ultimately destroy the value of the US dollar through "printing-press" currency inflation.

5) Defaults will scare away virtually all foreign capital, as will the falling dollar. Further US Treasury borrowing will thus be stymied.

6) Large classes of investors, such as "foreigners holding US debts", will act in markets homogenously. If asset prices fall, such as US Treasuries or US mortgages, there will be a lack of bargain hunting buyers to support prices at some level.

Actually, not one of these bold assumptions is true, though some have elements of truth. The following chapters will show why such broad generalizations cannot be an accurate reflection of a complex reality of millions of actors, and at the very least the effects Schiff is expecting will be dramatically dampened, making the hyperinflation threat highly unlikely, rather than the likelihood he claims.

As a note on terminology, I define "inflation" as simply "generally rising prices in terms of the common currency." This is the common understanding of the term. Oftentimes economists confusingly define inflation as an increase in the money supply, meaning 'inflated money supply' rather than 'inflated prices'. When I refer to "money supply inflation", I mean generally rising prices caused by an increased supply of money, which in modern economies is the exception rather than the rule. In Chapter Five, I show that the common assumption that an increased money supply must cause increased prices is deeply flawed.

But first, as a backdrop, I need to visit the concepts of economic value and economic activity. The bottom line in all economies is that the economy's participants will form their perceptions of economic value, and use their resources to enter into economic activities consistent with their personal perceptions of value and their needs or desires. In other words, people will simply spend or invest their money in a way that makes economic sense to them.[5]

---

5   The exception is those entrusted with others' money. Such fund managers may be sidetracked by other motives. This, unfortunately, has become a larger factor in moving markets in recent years with the growth in national wealth of the middle class and above. The proliferation of retirement accounts, and record performance of the stock market from 1982-1999, placed a lot of wealth into the hands of money managers who often seek short term performance (i.e. end of quarter results) that is at odds with sound risk/reward analysis investing. As a result, today's financial markets often have strong moves that are at odds with fundamental value; likely more so than in the past.

CHAPTER TWO

Economic Value and Economic Activity

ECONOMIC VALUE

Everything in economics ultimately boils down to the study of values. *Economics is a question of what human beings value, and to what degree.* The degree that one values something is represented by the price one would be willing to pay for it. In this way, the many individual actors in an economy come together in transactions (economic activity) when one party prefers to exchange some amount of what he has with something another party has, be it cash, goods, services, or securities.

All economic theories or predictions must ultimately hold up against a litmus test of the predictability of the perceptions of value of the majority of those who are setting the values through actual transactions. The question relevant for any prediction is, *"Is it reasonable to assume that by changing some variable in an economic system, that the majority of actors involved in that system will perceive the change in value in the predicted way?"* Oftentimes the answer is a resounding "no". Even when a population of completely logical actors would mean that yes, their perceptions and response should be predictable in direction. Consider the following, quoted from Warren Buffet, about how very "inefficient", or illogical, the auction rate bond markets can be:

"…we bid on three different Citizens securities that day. We got one bid at an 11.33% interest rate. One that we didn't buy went for 9.87%, and one went for 6.0%. It's the same bond, the same time, the same dealer. And a big issue. This is not some little anomaly, as they like to say in academic circles every time they find something that disagrees with their theory."[1]

There is no question that market prices at times make no sense, but often it is difficult to tell if there is in fact a good reason why prices are where they are. The same large bond issue sold on the same day varying by over 500 basis points, however, is pretty cut and dried. It clearly made no sense.

We will see that Schiff's reasoning presumes that large numbers of buyers and sellers making up specific markets will do the rational thing en masse. That's often not what happens, though, and is one source of breakdown of his theories that, at minimum, mitigate the extreme results he is predicting.

---

1   Varchaver, Nicholas. "What Warren thinks…", *Fortune* magazine, April 14, 2008.

Economic Activity

All economic activities are nothing more than transfers of some quantified values between parties. There is no economic activity that does not transfer some amount of something from a transferor to a transferee. Therefore, if no value exchanges hands, there has been no economic activity. Additionally, there can be no economic consequence from a lack of economic activity, except in cases where a lack of economic activity is a deviation from the norm. [2]

I encourage the reader to try to think of any possible exceptions to the above ideas. I believe there are none. Note that a change in quoted bid or ask price does not constitute an economic activity. It may change economic perceptions, but until that change in perception is acted upon in some transaction, there is no economic consequence. Similarly, if I post a "for sale" sign and price on my car's windshield, there is no economic activity or economic consequence until there is a buyer and a transaction. Until then it is simply a posted price which may be far too high to actually sell the car.

A main folly of economic thinkers such as Schiff

---

2   For example, if recurrent transactions between parties are the norm, then the ceasing of such transactions might have economic consequence.

17

occurs when they form broad conclusions having lost sight of the "street level" viewpoints, rational or not, of the actors on the two sides of every transaction. That is everything in understanding economics. If you could know absolutely everything about all market participants' perceptions of value; their motivations, opportunities and resources; you could predict economic activity and values (price levels). This applies to everything that is exchanged: stocks, bonds, commodities, currencies, wages, interest rates on loans, goods on store shelves, garage sale prices... you name it. Omniscience, of course, is not possible.

It is important to note that different people often would assign widely divergent values to the same thing. Items of nostalgia, or collectibles, are a good example. To some, a mint copy of the first 'Superman' comic book is a rare treasure and worth as much as *$1 million*, while to someone else it was not even worth saving after it was originally read. Or recently a 100 year old pair of Levi jeans was found in a California mine. I wouldn't pay $50 for such an antique, yet it was sold for over $36,000, and other antique denim fetches similar prices.

What is critical to gather from this is that values are completely based on perceptions, culminating in a supply and demand establishment of prices. *Scarcity* and *utility* are factored into perceptions. There may be a more or less 'consensus' on many types of goods' values, but there is no ultimate 'correct' truth to determine values. It is simply what buyers are willing to pay and sellers willing to sell for,

18

or 'what you can get for it'. It may be highly variable for some unusual, niche items, or hardly vary at all at a given time for simple, widely used 'commodities'. Perception is everything. You might view someone's valuation of something as completely irrational, yet his perception, which is quite different from yours, may be instrumental in setting the market's value.

But if there ever were an ultimate truth or benchmark of some type of bedrock value, the prize would have to go to gold. Gold was in fact the standard that backed the currency of many nations for centuries. Governments' currencies were redeemable for a fixed amount of gold or silver. In the case of the United States, gold was pegged at about $20 per ounce for over 100 years. That means that gold's value barely fluctuated at all, as citizens could redeem currency for gold at that rate from the government. However, even gold's value, treasured through millennia and across most cultures around the globe, has not *always* been deemed valuable, contrary to the gold bugs' insistence.

Many North American native tribes did not place much value on gold or silver. The history of the American West during the Gold Rush is replete with anecdotal evidence of Indians who had disdain for the white miners' obsession with the metals. There are many stories enduring to this day of Indians having had knowledge of valuable mineral deposits and deliberately hiding them forever, forgoing the opportunity of exploiting what they knew was of great value to the whites. They knew the easily gathered nuggets could be exchanged with the whites for great wealth in guns, horses and supplies, but even then most were not interested in the metal. Instead, they often buried these mineral deposits forever.

This demonstrates the power of differences in perceptions in assigning values, and that *even gold is only valuable because people think it is.* Gold bugs will scoff and say that gold is valuable because it is rare and beautiful, with unique metallic properties, and a unique history of being stable money during crises. These things are certainly true, but they are not the reason ultimately that gold is valuable. To illustrate, let your imagination go for an exercise:

Suppose there is an alien race that comes to visit earth, and they are disgusted with our materialistic ways. They are omnipotent, and they decide that to teach us a lesson to reflect on our materialism, they will make every gram of gold that was ever mined to become highly radioactive. Thus, getting anywhere near any gold becomes deadly. You would then have a situation where gold is still rare and beautiful, with all its unique metallic properties intact, and the illustrious monetary history, but by throwing in the new wrench of deadliness, it loses all its value. *This proves that those properties were not the reason it was valuable, but the belief was the reason.* Gold is valuable because people think it is, just as anything is valuable if people think it is, including paper money. That's why intrinsically worthless paper money has worked as long as it has.

If the belief is dislodged somehow, then the value fails. Of course, a rare commodity with intrinsic value, and especially gold, is far more solidly anchored psychologically than paper, should some earth-shaking event come along to test the faith. My point is that if the US dollar ever is to undergo hyperinflation, it will be a psychological phenomenon. Sure, other factors would come together to create the psychological sea change causing the hyperinflation, but as I pointed out earlier, perceptions are the key to value.

Therefore, the *only* ingredient necessary for a thing (i.e. currency) to be valuable is the shared, deeply entrenched belief that it is valuable. Should the belief fail, then the currency fails. Today it is quite true to say that Federal Reserve Notes are quite valuable. Virtually anyone passing a bill blowing on the street will rush to pick it up. What Schiff and gold standard proponents argue is that the day will come when that perception will be gone, lacking a gold or silver redeemability of the notes. Maybe that is possible one day, but the failure would come from a widespread *loss of faith*, and loss of faith alone.

'Perception being everything' does not just apply to tangibles and basic faith in money, but is just as relevant to valuation of securities in financial markets. A current example is the fact that when the US banking liquidity crisis came to a critical head in October 2008, the US dollar quickly rose a surprising 25% against most foreign currencies. Such a move in the dollar in such a short time was unheard of.

Of course the crisis was global in that foreign banks and stock markets were suffering the same devaluations as in the US, but for the dollar to rise at all is quite surprising. Fundamentals, such as surging US bad debts, US Treasury massive borrowing and spending,[3] and the record high US trade deficit with no sign of abating, all pointed to a *weakening* dollar. Yet the US, and particularly US Treasuries, were perceived by many to be a safe haven in the storm and thus the dollar gained a stunning amount against foreign currencies, and to date has held that gain. It makes no sense, as no fundamental forces supported a rising dollar, yet it rose with unprecedented strength.

All money is really just another commodity. I do not state this lightly. After thinking hard about it, and exploring the avenues such a thought leads to, I am convinced it is completely true. What separates money from other commodities is simply that money is given the special status of being the *standard* of exchange. A short history of United States money is in order:

In early colonial America, from a pure barter economy emerged tobacco, beaver pelts, nails and wampum (shell bead strings) as the standard 'monies', until later when coin became plentiful enough to be the standard. Coins were made of valuable metals so that the coins had intrinsic values to support the face value, even if melted down. Coins were viewed as lumps of so much copper, silver, or

---

3   expected to be inflationary to the dollar as well as causing concerns about the credit quality of the US Treasury

22

gold. Until 1857, foreign coins were legal tender in the US, and surprisingly outnumbered US coins by far in circulation! People didn't care too much which country had stamped the design, as the metal's value was what counted.

However, coins were not convenient for large transactions, and sometimes metal shortages in other parts of the world would create profit opportunities for melting and exporting them, causing domestic coin shortages. This, and economic growth in excess of what the coin supply could keep pace with, allowed paper money to have a place. As the law provided that Congress would enforce US money to be only of precious metal, the government did not originally issue paper money. However, private banks could. Congressional chartering of the "Bank of the United States" (precursor to the Federal Reserve) in 1791 got around that loophole, to provide a national standard currency to replace the dozens of free-wheeling private bank issued currencies. Paper money in those days was a note, or "I.O.U", payable on demand for gold or silver. The issuing bank would have in its vaults at all times, precious metal sufficient to retire all or part of its circulating notes. This guaranteed convertibility of paper money into gold is known as the gold standard.[4] "Gold bugs", such as Schiff, adhere to the notion that a gold standard resumption is

---

4   The "Classical" gold standard, common in nations before World War I, guaranteed convertibility of national paper money into gold on demand, at a fixed rate. The post-war, weaker "Gold Exchange" standard removed convertibility for individuals, but provided gold collateral between foreign governments holding each other's currency. Gold had been moved from private ownership to concentrated government stockpiles. In 1971, President Nixon retired the gold standard, removing all gold backing from Federal Reserve Notes.

necessary to avoid the inevitable financial catastrophe of unbacked fiat money. They say (ignoring the last several decades of our history) that money cannot be viable unless it has "intrinsic value" backing such as gold.

"Intrinsic value" refers to money that is useful, or valuable, even should the issuing authority or government (and consequently, faith) fail. A gold coin is still so many grams of gold, so it is valuable purely as a lump of metal. "Fiat", on the other hand, refers to money, such as paper money, that becomes worthless paper when the issuer fails. However, *perceptions of value*, as I have discussed, can even blur these cut and dried distinctions. For instance, the Confederate States of America's paper money became worthless when the Union won the Civil War, because the issuing government was defunct. However, a century later that fiat Confederate money of a defunct government was actually valuable once again as a collectible. All value is perceptions.

CHAPTER THREE

The 'Consumption is Waste' Myth

I try to be very careful with my words. If I use the word "myth", you can be sure I have dissected something with a lot of thought, and strongly believe that it lacks credibility. If I were not quite sure, I would not use such a strong term as "myth". I try to give the opposing camp the benefit of any doubt. But Mr. Schiff has been quite clear in his remarks that he finds consumption, or consumer spending, to be an unproductive waste for our economy. He states this in his first book—that consumption spending should not be included in GDP:

> "The problem is that most Americans, including most economists and investment advisers, have confused conspicuous consumption with legitimate wealth creation. Our impressive GDP growth, dominated as it is by consumption, is not a measure of how much wealth we have created, but of how much we have destroyed." [1]

He has typified what he considers consumption extravagance as such things as high-end home electronics, boats, second homes, vacations, and far too many unnecessary toys – often strung out on ill-afforded credit. To Schiff, tangible goods produced in factories, that can be exported, are an essential hallmark of a prosperous nation. He says

1 Peter Schiff with John Downes, <u>Crash Proof: How to Profit from the Coming Economic Collapse</u> (New Jersey: Wiley & Sons, Inc., 2007), 2.

the US consumption-based economy is illusory wealth.

His view of domestic consumption being a waste in terms of prosperity is shared by relatively few economists. I'd like to show it is untrue using an example that gives him the maximum advantage by being a completely frivolous way to spend money:

Suppose I take out a home equity loan just to have a wild party. I'm going to finance the whole thing for myself and a bunch of friends and blow all the money with nothing to show for it when it's done, but a debt and a hangover. Let's say I rent a fancy boat and crew for a week. I stock it with fine food, drink, supplies, and entertainment of all kinds, and we just sail out and party.

It is true that this is financial disaster for me personally. I now have zero value left of what I purchased, and a large debt plus interest to pay off. But what about to the economy? Is this an unproductive waste, or does it have some value?

It indeed has value because the dollars do not stop working once they are traded for boat and crew, food, wine, bait, and fuel. Those dollars are now enriching the pockets of the crew, bait shop, marina and liquor store. From there, some of those dollars may be spent on frivolous and fleeting pleasures, but some will not. And the spending cycle will continue on and on. *Even the dollars spent on frivolous things will always have the chance to be spent more productively by the next person.* Additionally, jobs are supported for the crew as well as the marina and shops. If enough people are enjoying the 'frivolous luxury' of sailing, the marina might expand and create more jobs. *All money that is spent by somebody is also received by somebody.* Schiff's error is in ignoring that every 'consumption' transaction has two sides, the consumption being only one of them. To the receiving party it is revenue and partially profit, which can fund business (or economic) expansion.

The portion that is individual income or business profit is then taxed by the government. Additionally, state sales tax is collected on most consumer purchases. *In this way, a portion of government stimulus spending always returns to the government by way of increased tax revenues.* It is the continuous spending/revenue cycle of individuals, businesses and governments that without a doubt has benefit to the economy in terms of more jobs, business profits, and tax revenues than would otherwise be. The faster the money cycle is moving from person to person (*the velocity of money*), the greater the economic benefit for the whole. This continuous cycling is the basic idea of economic stimulus. In this sense, it is entirely true to say that *money stuffed in the mattress (taken out of circulation) is the only money that is completely unproductive for the economy.*[2]

So money spent on unnecessary luxury or consumption definitely does add value to the economy, and in a valuable *multiplying ripple effect* as it endlessly travels from hand to hand. Additionally, the government recovers a piece of its 'stimulus spending' in income and sales

2   Money saved through investment is 'loaned out' and thus put back into circulation for productive use.

taxes every time the money changes hands.[3] It is surprising, and telling, that Schiff denounces the widely accepted economic principle of spending as a beneficial stimulus to an economy.[4] Few economic ideas are as clear to see as having validity, yet he scoffs at this as "phony" or "illusory" (consumption) wealth, unless it leads to exportable industrial production. It may be a waste for the spender if the value received is quickly consumed, but the revenue need not be wasted by the seller.

Let's say that I own a pet grooming boutique, and have a lucrative business selling grooming services. That 'illusory', frivolous wealth creation will be no illusion in my bank account, and I'll certainly enjoy spending some of it, thus creating cash flow and profits for other businesses as well. Thus my services do have a place in GDP. There is no illusion to the comfortable living that I am making, and my purchases stimulating other businesses, though you might think my services are spurious. Now Schiff would probably argue that is all about to change when foreigners stop buying American debts........."

But would it really change? And how would he know huge numbers of foreigners and central banks will unilaterally stop buying US Treasuries or securitized consumer debts? If they like exporting goods to Americans, they'll

---

3   Where consumption really is waste is in terms of the environmental cost, not to be confused with economic prosperity. From the environment's perspective, nearly all human consumption and capital investment tends to be a cost without benefit. It is important for future generations that we stop squandering our nonrenewable resources.

4   The spending part is surely of benefit; it's the cost part – in the case of government, the *taxes* and *borrowing* – that can be worrisome.

32

have to find somewhere to park all those dollars we send them. Read on and you will become increasingly skeptical of the Schiff scenario.

I have shown that even something as wasteful as 'partying' contributes to the economy, but let us suppose it did not. Even then, I will show that "the service sector" of which Schiff speaks as valueless, most definitely is valuable to our economy, and has a bona fide place in our GDP. Schiff has used "flipping hamburgers" as an example of an unproductive service sector job.

Let us assume Schiff is correct that only those people who drive the manufacturing base in this country are productive. So a US factory's production manager, a skilled line worker, a tool and die maker, and an engineer would all be valuable in terms of Schiff's true GDP. Wouldn't anyone who provides time-saving services to those people be contributing? How about the teacher of their children so they are freed from home schooling and can work more hours; the taxi driver when they are on a business trip; the restaurant that frees them from having to gather groceries and cook; their housekeeper; their auto mechanic? Every "service sector" person who provides data or information on the internet that is helpful to these "producers" in their specialty, has clearly made a contribution. All these services and myriads more are extensions of the most fundamental and time-tested economic principle of *specialization*, whereby the productivity of all individuals is multiplied by being freed from much time-consuming labor, both within and outside of their field.

In addition, the productivity multipliers we experienced first in 19th and 20th century industrialization and automation, and now in computer applications and the internet are really quite off-the-charts astounding. Although these advances require fewer people to do the work, what they can accomplish in a given time is incredible compared to the past. To bet against the US economy being productive and growing in light of these productivity multipliers I think is foolish. Of course the accompanying job loss from fewer people needed to perform the work is tragic, so many people without the requisite skills for these fewer jobs will be hurt.

But job loss is nothing new. Job loss has always been an inextricable part of progress. Tens of thousands of slaves built the great pyramids in Egypt, but today what would be the point? A few dozen guys with heavy equipment and cranes would do the trick. It is important to understand that is the reason we are so incredibly wealthy as a nation today. We have historically been the best society at utilizing innovation to vastly multiply human labor's efficiency and create wealth ever faster out of our rich resources, and with less labor. That benefit extends from the industrial age of the past to the information age of the present.

The United States has *pioneered* more innovation in our history than any other nation. That edge is not gone. We are the leader in technology, computer design and engineering, and the largest architect of information technology and the internet. Students from around the world continue to flock to the US to study in a great variety of disciplines from engineering to medicine because we have the best higher education in the world. These factors are the most potent "heavy equipment and cranes" of our time and a powerful growth force in mitigating any recession.

One distinct difference between our current recession, which many say will become a Depression (nobody knows this), and the 1930's is that in the Great Depression, people were genuinely "dirt poor". That term was popularized then. For many, the contracting economy and urban job loss meant going back to the farm and being largely self-sufficient. This labor–intensive way of life – *do-it-yourself because you couldn't afford to hire somebody* – made national economic recovery very slow in two ways. By families growing a lot of their own food, repairing their own equipment, mending clothes instead of buying new, et cetera, there was a lack of stimulative spending to fuel both private economic growth and government tax receipts. GNP fell an astounding 30% between 1929 and 1932. Businesses were folding right and left. At the same time that people were saving a lot in expenses by "do-it-yourself", they lost the time-saving benefit of specialization. They had to work long, hard days without the benefit and efficiency of hiring specialists to do the work.

The concept of specialization dictates that individuals' efficiency is multiplied by working within their specialties. Overall national productivity thus suffered in the

Great Depression because "do it yourself" is inefficient at producing value, as well as removes stimulative consumer spending from the economy. So it was true then and is true today that a skilled auto mechanic will get ahead faster by focusing on selling his expert labor fixing peoples' cars, rather than retire from his trade to make everything his family needs from scratch.[5]

This is a key difference why today's economy is much more resilient than during the Great Depression. Very few would attempt to "live off the land" today. Even flipping burgers would be more beneficial for the individual, and *much* more so for the economy, through the wage-spending-taxation cycle described earlier in this chapter. Through tremendous gains in productivity efficiency, many goods are now far cheaper, compared to even low wages, than they were during the Great Depression. Basic items, such as you would find at a 'dollar store', for example, can be purchased today for next to nothing where 80 years ago household items required a much more significant outlay, in terms of average wages. It is simply more efficient for nearly everybody today to work for even low wages to buy groceries, rather than attempt living off of gardening and raising chickens, once labor time is factored in. Thus, recessions now will see less contraction of GDP from voluntary consumer "withdrawal" of dollars from the open market economy, and this should mitigate the severity. The nature of our economy is that anytime money changes hands for

5   ...provided there are enough customers, which was a more likely problem during the 1930's.

goods or services, there is *stimulative benefit which at minimum is partially reflected in GDP.* Anytime spending is avoided by abstinence or "do it yourself", the stimulus benefit to the whole is foregone. There is a parallel in capital investment. Money that is deposited in a bank or invested is available for productive use in the economy, while money withdrawn and stashed away is unproductive.

A nation's prosperity, according to Schiff, comes largely from exporting to other nations. The idea apparently is that you get rich off the other guy's buying your stuff. This notion is completely flawed. Why couldn't a nation rich in resources become prosperous by developing those resources internally, never exporting a thing? The answer is that it certainly could.

"Most historians agree that the period in which the greatest [US] economic and technological progress occurred was between the end of the 18th century and the beginning of the 20th. During this period the nation was transformed from a primitive agricultural economy to the foremost industrial power in the world, with more than a third of the global industrial output. This can be illustrated by the index of total industrial production, which increased from only 4.29 in 1790 to 1975 in 1913, an increase of 460 times (base year 1850 - 100)."

The above quote is from an article at wikipedia.org entitled "Technological and Industrial History of the United States". I recommend reading its entirety. It details the United States' historical rise to the position as the world's foremost economic superpower, surpassing Britain, through natural resources and innovation. There is no mention of exports playing any role in that success. Other sources checked similarly depicted "The Gilded Age" in America without any credit given to exports.

Even the post World War II boom period, when Schiff has claimed specifically that exports were a key to our prosperity, is not remembered as a time of prosperity that was defined by booming exports in many historical accounts. Rich resources and innovation that multiplies productivity are the engines of wealth creation. Markets for products and services need to exist to attract profit-minded resource development, but those markets need not be across any border.

If you were to take Schiff's "trade surplus is the road to prosperity" theory and extend it from the level of "nation" to the level of "planet", it becomes obvious it does not work. *By this logic, the people of a planet, such as earth, would not be able to generate great prosperity unless they had a trade surplus with other planets!* I think we already know how that one turns out. Internal resource development and internal markets have funded all of earth's human prosperity, and internal resources and markets can and have also powered prosperous nations, such as the 19th to 20th century United States "Gilded Age". It simply is not necessary to have an industrial exporting base to be prosperous. Economists have been mulling over these things for decades and that is one axiom you won't find in the textbooks. There is no reason why the buyers need to live across any border. In your own line of work, have you found any special benefit to the company when the customer lives in a foreign land?

Aggregate national wealth creation comes from harnessing resources (natural resources, human labor and intelligence, and capital) and multiplying that by the power of the productivity efficiency that the economy has developed up to that point in time – i.e., the current level of technology. The beauty of this is that productivity efficiency, in both goods and services, continually marches on to higher levels. We call this "progress". If a new method is better, faster, or cheaper, it becomes adopted and society is enriched from better goods and lower prices, leaving more income for other things. As technology continually improves productivity efficiency, the nation collectively becomes richer *at a rate that increases over time.* Yesterday I bought an all-in-one printer that is far better than my old one in every respect, but cost only a third of what I spent on the old one. Inflation adjusted, it cost even less. I am better off, yet more cheaply, so I even have extra money to spend for myself and stimulate the economy.

But what about imports? Would imports somehow necessarily enhance or inhibit a nation's economy? After all, importing without any exports would be pure trade deficit. The nation would be sending money to foreigners in buying their goods, and never exporting to get any money back. This is a good question I deal with in Chapter Nine.

39

"It does not make any difference whether a country makes computer chips or potato chips."[6]

Schiff lauds manufactured goods' production as he decries unnecessary consumption. This raises the question of why the difference, and is there any real national 'wealth creation' difference between a durable manufactured good versus something quickly consumed, like food? If Schiff would applaud the production of automobiles as wealth-creation, then what happens in fifteen or twenty years when those cars are all used up and rusting out in the pasture? Where is the accumulation of national wealth that had been added once the cars are gone? He ignores the fact that all capital goods, plant and equipment, and productive 'wealth' have life cycles and depreciate eventually to worthlessness. The wealth is gone when the stuff is finally destroyed, crumbled or obsolete. Therefore, if manufactured "stuff" does not accumulate as national wealth over the very long term, Schiff's 'manufactured goods' theory of wealth does not explain the *exponential* growth in national wealth and annual production (GDP) the US has experienced steadily over the very long term.

Then the real difference between manufactured durable goods and fleeting goods such as food products, is simply the longer life cycle. Though it is true to say that

---

6   Michael Boskin, Chairman of the Council of Economic Advisers for President H.W. Bush; (Buchanan, Pat. "The Death of Manufacturing", *The American Conservative*, August 11, 2008).

food only maintains us and does not advance our net worth, *the same is true of durable goods like cars or televisions once their life cycle has run its course.* For the buyer of a meal, the cost of the meal is an immediate write-off to the wallet. For the buyer of a car, the cost of the car is not immediately lost, as the car has value, but that value will depreciate eventually to zero. For any asset that's value withers away (land or gold do not, for example), the enduring value of the asset's original production is therefore *not the asset itself. The enduring wealth created was the wages and profits earned from its production, which was added to the economic base.*[7] Since money can endure (through investment) and nearly all tangible assets depreciate, it therefore makes no difference from what type of good or service the profits and wages are derived.

Thus, as long as a worker has good pay, and as long as a business makes a good profit, they can thrive. Of course it's silly to prove such an obvious thing! It says nothing. But that's all we can really be certain about. We need to be careful and realize going any further down a path of predictions becomes increasingly speculative. We need to not get carried away by fantasies of imagined causation, or romantic ideals like domestic manufacturing being the holy grail to triumph over the import of cheap foreign goods. Schiff himself works in the 'service sector'– does he not think his investment services have any value to the nation? He says our service-based economy creates illusory wealth

---

7   Another component of enduring wealth is whatever new methodology was added to the sum total of human knowledge.

and that manufacturing is the real McCoy. Not so, as I have shown – it is in the profit where lasting wealth is added, not the stuff.

Another way to prove this is to follow the money and the goods. Schiff implies that manufacturing and exporting of goods define viable economic growth for a nation. But where are these 'truly valuable' exported manufactured goods once sold? They are all gone – shipped over the border. What is left to the producing nation is the profit, not the goods. If the goods are the wealth that was produced, and they are gone across the border leaving us only the profits, why would it matter if it was televisions we sold or intangibles like investment services or intellectual property? Either way this 'produced value' is sent away to the buyers.[8]

So if the nature of what a nation produces to sell doesn't matter, what does? It's so simple (and mundane) that you already know the answer. *What matters for an overall viable economy is that the goods or services that the businesses produce have sufficient demand to keep the businesses profitable.* Unprofitable businesses will sooner or later fail. (Mass failures across the whole economy are of course a devastating problem.) Profitable ones will continue to provide goods or services on one hand and employment on the other – thus viability.

---

8   If anything, exporting intangibles such as 'consulting services' would be *preferable* to selling manufactured goods. 'Knowledge' assets are not simply gone to the buyer, but are retained as well. Goods also are disadvantageous in requiring certain amounts of material, energy and shipping costs with every unit sold.

I expect the reader is looking for an explanation of national prosperity less mundane and obvious – something intriguing and profound, a romantic ideal! People are naturally uncomfortable with uncertainty. They want answers, predictions – something to believe in which will provide security, and direction for investing. Good luck with that!

I'm afraid if you seek explanations more exciting than that, what you'll get will just be somebody's speculation, such as an 'Exported goods vs. Wasteful Consumption' theory of prosperity. Who can predict future demand and price levels of millions of products and services across a vast economy? Who will even know what new products and services will dot the landscape several years from now, or how competition will change? Everybody knew by the late nineties that the internet would revolutionize how we do business and be a huge economic growth engine, but almost nobody had any vision then of how exactly the internet would unfold.

Similarly, we know we had a real estate bubble and many were overly leveraged – consumers and financial institutions alike. We know there will be a price to pay for all the unchecked government borrowing. But nobody knows how bad it will get and how it will play out. *Be wary of those who know!*

In this chapter, I have addressed the myth that spending on consumption is without economic value. I return to my points of Chapter 2 on economic value. Value is in the eye of the beholder. Whether goods or services are being sold does not matter. As long as there is healthy demand for the output of the economy, domestically or from abroad, the fundamentals of the economy will be healthy.[9] This is because healthy sales will allow businesses to remain profitable and employment high. Meeting the demand profitably is the key for success, then, not the nature of the goods or services being demanded and produced.

---

9   ...notwithstanding the case of excessive leverage leading to high defaults. Even this will only cause temporary recession if demand remains relatively sound. Schiff's scenario depends on demand for our non-exportable 'service sector' economy plummeting when, he claims, Americans' wealth will be crushed by a combination of excessive debt, fallen paper asset values, rising unemployment and a fallen dollar.

CHAPTER FOUR

Why a Dollar Plunge Would Self-Correct

Schiff sees the unavoidable "printing press" solution of the government as causing a rapid hyperinflationary spiral. He assumes the *amount and speed* of public reaction to additional money supply would be, in fact, sufficient for the most extreme version of inflation – hyperinflation. This view is purely speculation. I will not say it is impossible, as many remotely improbable things are in the realm of the possible, but he offers little detail or quantitative analysis for that very extreme conclusion. He gives only a most generalized thread of causation in how hyperinflation would come about: the inability of the US Treasury to borrow any more from foreigners = maximal Fed printing of currency[1] = hyperinflation. If the Treasury does suffer some lack of buyers of its new debt issues, the links in this chain of events are far from strong. Also, there are a number of mitigating factors he ignores, including time itself. Those equals signs are quite tenuous. There would certainly be some degree of a number of self-correcting forces supporting and at minimum, slowing, a falling dollar. Very little slowing effect would be needed to curtail super-fast 'hyperinflation'.

Though the US stock market has fallen some 40% in

---

1 "Printing of currency" is literal or figurative to Schiff. In *Crash Proof: How to Profit from the Coming Economic Collapse*, Schiff explains that his definition of "printing currency" includes non-currency monetary easing by the Fed. This could lead to much new money supply in the form of credit — bank balances, etc.

the last year, we must remember that it took many months of trading down and breaking through support levels for this to occur. Even so, a 40% fall in 12 months is not at all analogous to hyperinflation. Hyperinflation is more like a 40% loss of value in the US dollar in a matter of hours. Then instead of a rally or basing reaction to the sudden fall, such staggering losses would follow each other day after day in hyperinflation. Loss of faith in the currency is so extreme that there are *zero* bargain hunters who, attracted to a lower value, would come in with buying support at the lower currency exchange rates. In the case of the US dollar, Schiff is implying that virtually no foreign currency holders or speculators will want to trade for dollars or buy US dollar denominated assets at any level and thus slow the fall.

Considering that the US dollar is the world's reserve currency, used for central bank reserves and trade of many nations, and the most widely privately held currency, it is a great stretch to say that all these millions of foreign investors (including exporters to the US and central banks) will come to the same conclusion together that the US dollar is completely worthless and unilaterally dump them, while getting virtually nothing in return for them since their value had plunged.

If indeed many dollar holders begin to form the conclusion that the US economy and dollar are seriously weakening, the reasonable result would be that the US dollar will trade lower over time in a more prolonged decline. How much lower and longer is anybody's guess, but it's not going to lose 95% of its value in a week. At least there is no sound reason to believe it would, based on Schiff's cause being the excessive printing of currency. One reason is that as dollars become (more gradually) cheaper, dollar denominated goods (including securities) become more attractive to those holding foreign currency. So US real estate, stocks, bonds, hard assets, and exports all start looking like better buys to foreigners the more the dollar declines against their currencies.[2] *This increase of foreign demand will serve to support prices for all these things, as well as stimulate the US economy, thus stemming the dollar (or the US economy) decline from any rapid implosion.* Schiff implies that the opposite is true – that the more the dollar falls against say the yen, the less attractive American US dollar-ed assets are to the Japanese. This is obviously fiction. Even if they fear holding dollars for some reason, they will recognize the dollars have value for the American goods they can *presently* buy. They will buy dollars, getting a lot of them for their yen, and if afraid of holding the dollars can trade them quickly for US hard assets at prices they will have already ascertained in the markets. The falling dollar will not scare foreigners away; it will entice them.

---

2   It can be argued that theoretically prices' inflating perfectly in counterbalance of the falling currency will cancel out this asset 'bargain hunting' opportunity, but in reality not all prices can adjust universally and instantaneously to inflation (or a falling currency, which can be considered inflation). We recently saw the dollar climb some 25% against most currencies in a matter of weeks. But prices of most US goods did not symmetrically and sympathetically fall over that period, so currency changes do not have to be accompanied by a domestic corrective price inflation (or deflation). It is common knowledge that currency exchange rates usually simply make or break opportunities to bargain hunt in other countries. *So a falling dollar will increasingly attract foreign currency demand for cheap dollars and dollar-denominated assets.*

For a specific example, suppose Mexican food producers are looking to buy wheat for tortillas. If the dollar drops in half against the peso, then Mexican pesos now buy twice as much wheat as they did.[3] Suddenly American wheat is more competitive in the international markets, and the Mexicans will exchange pesos for US dollars to repatriate for American wheat, regardless of how they feel about the dollar. It's a matter of economics that where value increases in relation to cost, buying support comes in. Thus with a falling dollar against other currencies, US exports undoubtedly would gain volume, US imports decline, and US investment asset prices in general receive support. Foreigners will also travel in the US to use their extra purchasing power, thus stimulating the US economy further. These are desirable self-correcting consequences that Schiff has failed to acknowledge. They not only support a falling US dollar, but they decrease the US trade deficit, while stimulating the US economy.

A more reasonable view than hyperinflation would be that unchecked printing of greenbacks might cause some serious inflation, albeit more gradually. Let's give Schiff maximum benefit of the doubt and say that in desperation the Fed creates a very large increase in the money supply. It's anybody's guess, but *suppose* as a result we get historic annual inflation of around 50%. Even this extreme inflation

---

3 US wheat would have had to double in price in domestic inflation to negate this benefit to Mexican buyers. Typically, US goods prices *do not* adjust in step and in counterbalance to US dollar fluctuations, so the opportunity for peso holders is likely to be real during a dollar decline.

would need not progress to hyperinflation. *What hyperinflation would require is widespread loss of faith that the US dollar was worth anything at all.* Only then would people be willing to trade buckets of currency for some small purchase, as in the Weimar Republic. During hyperinflation, people prefer holding any kind of goods to the currency, as the currency loses substantial value in even a single day. A barter system (or other currency with greater faith) would come to prevail as the dollar would be completely dead in people's minds.

So a more gradually falling dollar would indeed encourage US investment from foreigners, but what about a sudden and massive plunge from *ubiquitous loss of faith* in the currency itself? This is truly the only scenario that could send the dollar completely through any buying support – virtually everybody losing all faith at once. It is only hypothetical and unimaginable in the world today. But what if such a thing could happen?

Then it would also require the theoretical case of there being no goods readily available in US dollars that are worth buying. If valuable assets can still be bought by some amount of dollars, then dollars have to have value if for no other reason than to quickly be used to buy those assets. This provides support for a fallen dollar. In other words, if a foreign party believes the dollar will become worthless, but realizes that in the meantime some desirable goods can be purchased with some amount of dollars because a US seller does not yet think the dollar will become worthless, then the party can buy dollars to quickly spend on the goods before the dollar declines. It is a sort of quick arbitrage opportunity that would provide some support to a severely falling dollar. *In essence, there has to be value to the dollar as long as it can still purchase something of value.* So if all US real estate, all US sound and profitable businesses, and all US privately and publicly owned goods, services and securities of all kinds cannot be purchased with even large amounts of dollars, then the US dollar is in deepest trouble. Not likely! The psychological tipping point of nobody being a seller at even very high prices in US dollars would be incredibly hard to reach in such a vast economy.

Schiff has also claimed that the US will be cut off from its current supply of cheap, imported foreign goods. He seems to argue that foreign manufacturers will view the US dollar as poison, and simply stop selling to Americans for US dollars, which could only be used by them to purchase US (bad) debts. He says the resulting shortages will contribute to inflation, pinching consumers harder, and resulting in a great, expanded market for second hand goods. Schiff has depicted this in *Crash Proof: How to Profit from the Coming Economic Collapse* - that America will become like a vast second-hand store.

This makes no sense in the real world. If you put yourself in the shoes of a foreign manufacturer, you have every incentive to sell to the US and ceasing to do business with America would be harming yourself. Suppose I am a Korean textile manufacturer that sells apparel to US department stores. If the dollar falls 50% over a period of weeks or months against the South Korean won, would I stop selling to US department stores, or would I just offer my goods at double the prices to reflect the changing currencies? The answer is obvious – rather than idle the factory and lose money, I will be motivated to continue production and sales, and simply adjust my price to the new currency exchange rates. The sales dollars I receive can be quickly exchanged for Korean won if I fear there is future risk in holding dollars. But if today the dollar is half of its value of six months ago against the won, I would only be hurting myself to halt production and sales to the US. If the dollar falls another 50%, I can double my prices again. I will not voluntarily refuse to sell for dollars, but will simply require more of them to make it worth my while.

This effect of a lower dollar is that it becomes more expensive for Americans to import foreign goods. This will eventually curtail US imports and create incentives for US manufacturers to move production back to the US (also saving the cost of transporting goods half way around the world). So a devalued dollar would no doubt eventually have the positive side effect of decreasing the US trade deficit and stimulating US manufacturing. Isn't more US manufacturing and jobs what we want? A declining dollar at some level will make that shift attractive enough.

Yes, the current trade deficit means that foreigners are selling to us more than we sell to them, resulting in net dollars flowing overseas. But then the foreigners must invest the US dollars somehow. They don't want to hold US currency that pays no interest. The Koreans can't spend dollars at local businesses where the won is the only medium of exchange. They can exchange the dollars for won, but now the new recipient either has to hold the US currency (earning no interest) or park them in US assets of some kind. *This is a tremendous support for the US investment market, especially US Treasuries.* The fact that the US dollar holds the unique position as the world's reserve currency enhances this greatly. Many foreign nations and businesses must hold a lot of US dollars as a practical matter, and whoever does a lot of exporting to the US will be receiving a lot of US dollars. There is no way around it.[4]

Foreign US dollar holders' only choices are to spend them on US goods, services or investments, or hold them as US currency which earns no interest. In this way the US trade deficit has the great benefit of *continually* putting a lot of dollars overseas, which come back to the US as demand for US Treasuries, in large part, because Treasuries are believed to be safe and they pay some interest. This is a raw deal for foreigners, but quite good for the US to be supplied with nearly limitless capital at the cheapest interest rates on earth. *As long as foreigners have a profit incentive to export to the US, they will do so.* Then they will have to park the dollars they receive somewhere – in US assets or simply by holding US currency.

---

4   This is borne out by the fact that the Federal Reserve estimates that the majority of the aggregate value of Federal Reserve Notes in circulation are actually outside the US.

If a foreigner decides that US Treasuries and the dollar are risky and likely to fall because he thinks our economy is failing, he will trade his holdings in dollars for another currency. If he swaps with another foreigner, it makes no difference to the US. The same amount of US dollars is abroad after the swap. If he instead redeems the dollars to somebody in the US in exchange for either goods or foreign denominated investments, the effect is a *reversal* of that much value of US trade deficit. In other words, dollars changing hands overseas matters not to the US – it's just one foreigner holding them versus another. But dollars coming home to the US and leaving foreign circulation altogether are necessarily redeemed for US held assets of some sort. This is an act of US trade surplus, and thus a reduction of our trade deficit. This foreign demand does not hurt the US economy.

If every US dollar in foreign hands came back to the US in exchange for US assets, it would simply reverse the accumulated trade deficits from over the years. Those dollars are claim checks for US assets. If foreigners never spent their dollars back in the US, the effect is that the US (dollar) economy is effectively simply expanded over the borders – that's all. *The US economy, effectively, is not the economic activity that occurs within US borders. It is the economic activity that occurs anywhere in US dollars.* In this way the trade deficit is not a prosperity problem, except in terms of US job losses.

"The U.S. economy comprises not only its domestic base but also the many foreigners who invest in the U.S. one way or another. The greater the fraction of their assets that foreigners hold in dollars, the more their financial well-being depends on a strong dollar. Ultimately they will become full members of the U.S. economy. That they may live overseas is no longer relevant."[5]

The foreign exporters who choose to accept and hold US dollars or dollar-based securities, have simply opted to be part of the US dollar economy. A producer in China that sells products exclusively to the US, only in US dollars, is in essence no different from that same producer moving his production to the US and selling us the same wares. The significant difference is the cheap production cost in China, and the difference in the location of jobs.

When Schiff says foreigners will become disenchanted with US dollars, driving the dollar's value down, there's absolutely nothing they can do to get rid of them (in the aggregate) but to dump them back in the US. This demand will bolster the US economy and exports in particular. The trade deficit would decrease and perhaps turn to a surplus. *When any currency gets killed against others, holders of the currency who hope to convert some portion of it into another currency pay a big price. Holders of the fallen currency who will only be exchanging the currency for assets denominated in that currency are not directly affected.* Therefore,

5   William Hummel, "The Trade Deficit", Money: What it Is, How it Works, 25 Aug 2006, 17 Dec 2008, http://wfhummel.net/tradedeficit.html

if the US dollar drops, US residents who do no business and have no assets in other currencies suffer no direct currency effect. Dollar holders who wish to convert them to another currency will suffer. Foreign holders of US dollars and US citizens will therefore both have an incentive to buy dollar-denominated assets in the US rather than receive a poor foreign exchange rate buying non-US assets.

So let's say the US economy is tanking and the dollar is falling sharply, and this causes foreigners to want to dump them, as Schiff predicts. Whatever they dump to other (foolish) foreigners doesn't change the number of dollars in foreign hands. But suppose no foreigner wants them so they have to spend them in the US to get some value before they drop even further. Considering that trillions of US dollars are foreign held, including those in the form of US debts, this great unwinding's resulting increased demand for US over Asian goods and assets would actually be a huge boon for the US economy. Exports would leap as imports fell.

Suppose Walmart buys shirts made in Indonesia for $2 each, but then the dollar drops by 50%. Suddenly it is not worth it to the Indonesian factory to sell shirts to Walmart for less than $4, with the currency exchange rate being the sole change. If imports continue to get more expensive because the dollar is falling, at some point it makes sense for American companies to manufacture here again rather than half way around the world.

This is where Schiff says we will have a "long and

painful" rebuilding of our manufacturing base. He doesn't give particular reasons why it would be long and costly, which I find doubtful. *Though the US manufacturing sector is only one third of the portion of the US economy that it was fifty years ago, it is far from gone.* Much of our 'imports' also come from production on foreign soil that is or was once actually US owned or operated. The chief historical reason for moving production abroad was cheap labor and sometimes international trade incentives. The US manufacturers have not lost the production know-how, and in fact have pioneered and developed CAD/CAM technology. It should not be especially difficult, if the dollar has little purchasing power for imports, to just purchase and ship the equipment to the US and renovate old factories to produce again. It is also amazing how fast new construction takes place these days, so I do not see the long, painful depressionary rebuilding period that Schiff claims will be. Schiff himself says that service sector jobs will shrink. This would create a ready and reasonably priced labor market to fill any new manufacturing jobs.

In summary, a declining US dollar, which some say is certain as net dollars continue to flow overseas, will not decline anywhere near as fast as in hyperinflation due to money supply excesses because in our economy there are mitigating factors that would simply have to slow the fall. The foreign (currency) exchange market has vast numbers of traders with differing strategies and beliefs that would prevent an "all selling" complete free fall scenario from destroying the dollar in a short time. Buying support at some point would stretch out a fall over a longer term, much like the stock markets of 2008. In addition, certain fundamental positives for the dollar come into play as it declines, supporting it. Namely, better deals for those holding foreign currency to buy dollars to purchase American assets and trade that begins to favor American exports over imports. At the same time, foreign exporters would not "stop" selling to Americans, but would simply raise prices to adjust for the dollar's decline. Thus, the demand from abroad for dollars, and consequently dollar denominated assets and investments, would also not simply cease.

Sure, if virtually all foreigners holding US dollars could have utterly certain convictions, within a short time, that the US dollar is *completely worthless*, the resulting stampede selloff could decimate the dollar permanently. However, such conviction would not make any fundamental sense, regardless of any money supply increases, and cannot realistically happen. With so many minds involved, and greed intermingling with fear during sharp declines, there is sure to be uncertainty and enough contrarian support to prolong and level off any fall.

CHAPTER FIVE

Inflation by Way of the Money Supply

Schiff claims that the only way politicians can ultimately respond to the inevitable economic downward spiral is by "the printing press". In other words, they will fund the massive debt service and deficits, once the Treasury can no longer borrow, by increasing the money supply – simply printing more money and creating credit money supply. The short-sighted advantage to the government in the (supposed) resulting inflation would be that high inflation is great for those in debt, and nobody is in debt like the US Treasury! If the Treasury could pay off today's national debt years from now with cheap, super-inflated dollars it would benefit greatly and could actually easily pull off retiring the national debt (see Chapter Eight). In fact, Schiff argues that the government will have no choice but to induce such inflation. However, this would be foolish for the government as such tremendous inflation (which is essentially destruction of the dollar) would be ruinous to the US economy. I certainly don't argue with Peter on that.

There is more than one potential cause for inflation.[1] I will differentiate between three types of inflation that I call *money supply inflation, cost-push inflation*, and *creeping inflation*. Schiff's view is that money supply inflation

---

1 For purposes of this book, the term "inflation" always means "generally rising prices". I never use "inflation" to mean many economists' technical definition of "inflated (increased) supply of money", which creates confusion to the layperson. My term "money supply inflation" refers to generally rising prices caused by an increased money supply.

will be our culprit, and surely lead to hyperinflation. I will demonstrate that for money-supply inflation to be high, and thus a problem, *certain conditions must exist.* Schiff's view presumes, on the other hand, that a large money supply increase necessarily must cause a large amount of inflation. He and many economists seem to consider money supply inflation as a somewhat predictable foregone conclusion, like mathematics or a natural law. This is false!

For example, in an electrical circuit, if you increase the voltage (electrical pressure), there is increased current flow proportional to the increased voltage. This is a mathematical, natural law in a simple system, though. You're only dealing with three things that always behave the same, simple, completely predictable way every time: voltage, amperage and resistance. Increasing the US money supply by 15% by simply "printing money" does not mean that prices and wages will sympathetically inflate by 15%. They might not rise at all. Consider these examples:

First let's look at a similarly simple system to an electrical circuit in a tiny economy. Let's say that a poker game of ten players is a little economy. Each player is issued 100 chips for $100 (a buck a chip) and that it is all the money allowed in this game. Also, one chip will buy a beer (the host is too cheapskate to provide!). After a while, some players are down quite a bit and worried about losing so fast and being sidelined, so the host comes around and gives all ten players 100 more chips for free. Since only $1000 is still in the kitty to distribute to chip holders at the end of the game, obviously the 2000 chips in the game can only be worth 50 cents each now. Also, the host is not dumb, so now a beer will cost 2 chips.

What just happened is *money supply inflation.* By doubling the money (chip) supply, it now takes 2 chips to equal what 1 chip used to represent. A beer went from costing 1 chip to 2 chips, yielding an inflation rate of 100%, as the chip value dropped 50%. In the poker game example, though, this money-supply inflation is fair and agreeable to all. *It is a sort of perfect inflation because it is has the same net result as no inflation at all.* Each chip has lost half of its value, but nobody gains or loses from the inflation. Let us see why.

Don't get me wrong – I'm not suggesting that money-supply inflation in the real world doesn't hurt people and economies, as it can be devastating. But the reasons nobody is hurt by chip inflation in the poker game is that the increased money supply is distributed in complete equality to all without any cost or effort, and the vendor of beer knows the amount of new money (chips) in the system and can adjust his price exactly accordingly. This never happens in any real economy. Inflation can never occur in equal amounts simultaneously for all wages and prices in a complex, free economy. The newly printed money is not acquired without effort or simply distributed equitably to all.

Here is another example of money supply inflation, but getting a little more complex and realistic, to illustrate a few points:

Suppose there is a primitive village along a river by the ocean. Every year there is a salmon run up the river, and for several weeks the villagers can harvest the bounty of the salmon for food. They also use the salmon as a medium of exchange, or money. During the salmon run, the fish are easily caught by wading, and some enterprising souls catch many extra fish to use as money to trade for various goods. Excess fish can be smoked, dried and stored for winter food.

Some years the salmon are very plentiful and other years they are sparse. In a lean year, 1 fish may buy a nice flint knife. However, in a year when the fish are abundant it may require 5 fish to buy the same piece of flint. In fact, in some years if the villagers become inundated with super plentiful fish, raw fish may no longer serve as currency. The fish-wielding buyer of goods may have to add value by adding his labor of smoking the fish before anyone will take them.

This illustrates in a more realistic but simple economy how money supply inflation could work. When fish (money) are scarce, the price of a flint might be 1 fish. When fish are more plentiful, the increased money supply causes price inflation, and a flint might cost 5 or 10 fish. Increased money supply alone caused this inflation. When fish are so abundant that the villagers have more than they can possibly use in the village, there is high inflation and the value of fish money moves toward zero. You can hardly pry a flint knife out of anybody's hand with any amount of fish.[2]

In this economy, of course, a wide panoply of items are routinely traded for the currency of fish, not just flint knives. There is direct barter of items without using fish, too. Naturally, prices vary quite a bit because at any given time during the salmon run season, nobody knows whether their numbers will by steady, increase or decrease during the remainder of the run. There are surges of fish money when many entrepreneurs are actively fishing, driving up prices. Sometimes villagers are willing to pay a bit more for the convenience of getting fish from the first fisherman that comes around even if it costs, say, a little extra firewood (like buying a snack at a high price at the convenience store). There are qualitative differences in flint knives, fish, and other goods, too. There is uncertainty about the future fish supply tomorrow or next week, and there is unequal knowledge for different villagers of the latest 'economic' fish news. There is so much uncertainty that prices can vary widely day to day, sometimes hour to hour, or from one end of the village to the other. Pricing has much element of guesswork, and the fish supply (today's catch) and today's fish demand around the village are not known to all equally. A few are "in the know" on a daily basis but most just assume today's fish supply is probably about the same as yesterday's.

The village that uses fish money is not at all like the

---

2 The only way is sell 'fish futures' on next year's catch!

poker game analogy because of the many complexities and an *imperfect awareness of the money supply*. However, it is fair to say that on any given day, there is some typical range of value for the fish currency in terms of flint. In a plentiful fish year, maybe 7-12 salmon per knife is about right, while in a really lean year 2-5 might be reasonable. In other words, markets fluctuate in a relatively narrow range short term, and may drift in a wider range over a longer term. Imperfect awareness, changing supply, and uncertainty create a fluctuating value for fish currency, unlike the poker chips. The poker chips' value does not change unless new supply is introduced, while the fish money's value tends to wander, creating a "market" for the currency not unlike the market for the US dollar.

Both short and long term market trends can be very difficult to predict. It is sometimes relatively easy to gauge probabilities (over the long term) of direction, but not degree. For example, I think it is extremely likely that 10 years from now oil prices will be much higher than today's $40 per barrel. But having to predict the actual range would be futile. Will it be closer to $100, $150, or more a barrel? It's pure speculation, even to an expert who studies the long term projected demand, supply and costs of production. All three projections can easily change a lot.

The very, very few who can consistently predict market trends just 60% of the time or better can become extremely rich. Seventy percent accuracy for a stock picker is excellent. Schiff has indicated he is certain about something that is incredibly rare (hyperinflation), and would be a massive turning of our world upside down.[3] I would take him more seriously if he said he gave hyperinflation a 20% probability. *His relative certainty just makes it all the more likely he is modeling the US and global economies far too simply in his mind.*

As we move from the simple fish-currency village scenario to the modern US economy, contemplating how the nation and the world would react to a greatly increased US money supply becomes so complex, with millions of price and wage setters theoretically trying to adjust, that it is completely unknowable. For Schiff to make simplistic cause and effect assumptions about the money supply "printing press" and hyperinflation (like my electrical circuit), is simply not realistic. Even his presumption that foreign buying of US Treasuries will dry up and force the government to print money of the magnitude he suggests is speculative (see Chapter Eight). Additionally, the degree of any price inflation caused by even a large money supply increase would probably be mitigated a lot by imperfect perceptions and simple human inertia. In such a vast economy, it wouldn't surprise me at all if the Fed were to increase the money supply substantially and nobody but bankers and Fed-watchers really noticed! There won't be cashiers giving out extra dollars with people's change because there is all this extra easy money floating around! Can you picture a

---

3   On his Dec. 17, 2008 radio show, Schiff said that due to the Federal Reserve's course of action he was now certain that the US dollar would be destroyed by hyperinflation, sooner rather than later.

few years from now currency blowing around in the streets because it is not worth picking up, like pennies today? This would be the outcome of hyperinflation. If you think the government borrowing massively and printing money will have this affect on main street's perceptions any time soon, then you underestimate both our economy and Americans' faith in the fiat money that has, in fact, worked just fine since 1965.

Schiff is a charismatic, smart and very articulate guy, and he did predict the popping of the real estate bubble and subprime crisis, but a worthless dollar is pretty far-fetched. The difference in the predictions is enormous. Seeing the rapidly soaring home values and understanding the rotten lending and securitization racket that was propping them up is sort of like predicting the outcome of a game when it is the bottom of the ninth inning with 2 outs and the score is 10 to 1. It's just that most economists and policy makers weren't paying much attention to that game at the time. They didn't take a hard look at the new subprime lending and securitization practices. On the other hand, predicting not just high inflation, but extreme and very rare hyperinflation, due to the current government's stimulus spending and its eventual monetary solution to the burgeoning debt is more like forecasting today all the winners of the World Series for the next several years.

When interest rates change, the media hangs on every word of the Fed and people quickly see these changes affect their borrowing rates, money market yields, bond prices, etc., but money supply changes are quite under the radar for almost all of us. For increased money supply to really cause inflation, it would have to be filtered through the economy to take effect. There could be dramatic mitigation of its effect along the way. For example, if the Fed would increase the M2 money supply 25% over the course of a year through easing and printing, nobody can truly say how much it would affect price inflation. Actual inflation experienced might be 10%, or zero. Nobody really knows, and there is no predictive model that works. Inflation is very hard to even measure, as price changes vary so much across various classes of goods and geographically. The published change in CPI level can be quite different from what different consumers actually experience in the prices of things they personally buy. In recent years, health care, tuition, housing and certain government services have had large cost increases, but items such as computers, electronics and clothing have become much cheaper. McDonald's "dollar value menu" is still the "dollar value menu" after decades, so inflation spares some things. Productivity gains in production often overcome inflation, so prices of many things fall in real terms. Additionally, current fears of deflation persisting during this economic contraction could partially offset any money supply inflation.

Adding to the difficulty (impossibility, really) of predicting how a given increase in money supply might ultimately translate into an inflation figure, is the fact that currency (Federal Reserve Notes and coins), makes up only a small fraction of the money supply that we use. Most of our money is in bank balances that are purely representational credit and have no corresponding currency sitting in any vault. For every $1 in savings, checking, money market and bank CD accounts, there is only about 10 cents worth of coin and currency in existence 'backing' it.[4] Thus, for every $1 in bills and coins in circulation, there is currently roughly $10.41 in 'money supply' that powers our day to day economy. This is because most money, especially larger transfers, is only in the form of account balances, not coin or currency. No actual bills are needed for larger transfers, as we all know from our daily transactions. Thus, if the Federal Reserve had some way to print and inject a doubling of the currency that is in circulation, the M2 money supply would only jump by around 10%! This alone makes high inflation from any literal printing of bills in our economy unlikely, even in grim financial times when the public might tend toward being skeptical of money's value. Currency is simply too small a part of our money supply to drive inflation all the way to the extreme of hyperinflation very effectively.[5] Over ninety percent of our cash money (M2) exists simply as balances in accounts. So "Helicopter Ben" Bernanke would

---

4   The Federal Reserve's "M1" measure of basically ready transactional money is made up of currency (including coins) in the public's hands and checking (demand) deposits. The broader M2 measure also includes savings accounts, CD's below $100,000 and money market accounts. As of November 2008, the Fed reported circulating currency (and coin) of $761 billion. This currency figure comprises 52.9% of the M1 money supply, and just 9.6% of the M2 money supply.

5   Minting of new coins does not increase the money supply as the Treasury sells the coins to banks (through the Federal Reserve) at face value. Therefore currency is retired equal to the value of coins issued.

need some serious flying time in the chopper to add a big percentage to the money supply via currency drops![6]

To be fair, gold bugs speak of massive "printing" of money in both a literal and figurative sense. Since far more money exists in the form of credit (bank balances) than as currency, the potential for 'credit' money supply creation through easing interest rates and Fed open market purchases is far greater than simply printing currency. I'll address money supply increases by credit creation through Fed policy momentarily. First, we need to look at how money is actually created in our economy:

When a bank needs more currency to meet customer demand or as reserves for making new loans, it orders the currency from the Federal Reserve. *The Fed does not initiate these orders, but only responds to the private banks' demands for currency.* When it sends the requested new currency to the bank, it debits that bank's account at the Federal Reserve. Thus a liability is created to balance the currency sent to the bank, so that the currency is not 'free' for the bank. The Fed does not consider this new money sitting in the bank's vault to be part of the public 'money supply' yet, until it actually leaves the vault and is in the hands of the public.[7] So bank vaults essentially act as an extension of the Federal Reserve's currency 'warehouse' for distribution purposes, keeping the cash at the ready for the

6   Fed Chairman Ben Bernanke's speech of November 21, 2002 on deflation invoked a notion of Milton Friedman that the government could always drop money from helicopters if it had to. The passing mention has unfairly given Bernanke the moniker of "Helicopter Ben".

7   This is a reasonable view.

public.

However, this newly printed currency in the bank vaults cannot be forced on the public to "increase the money supply", even if that were a government goal. *Rather, the banks themselves create new money (in the form of credit) by writing new loans. The banks actually can cut their borrowers the loan checks out of thin air!*[8] This may seem like some kind of clever trick thinking to disguise the truth, but I assure you it is not. The reason such ridiculously easy money creation out of thin air doesn't result in catastrophic inflation is the fact that *the money is not "easy" to you, the borrower.* It comes with big strings attached, called "interest" and "principal" to be repaid in the future. This high psychological cost keeps the value of this money high and from hyperinflating, though the actual cost to the bank of producing the money is nil. This also shows how perception is truly value.

The bank's new vault currency is then distributed only to the extent that the borrower wishes to convert the new loan to currency. So new currency is not pushed from the Federal Reserve out into the economy. Rather, it is pulled by the public. As you can see, the Federal Reserve can print all the money it wants, but the normal banking system does not allow for the government to force currency out into the money supply. This may seem strange, but it is absolutely true. Indeed, the public normally controls the

---

8 Banks can do so for borrowers up to about 10 times the amount of capital that the bank actually has. A borrower's loan is not matched up as a transfer against somebody's deposit.

size of the money supply by borrowing and the Fed just reacts to ensure there is adequate currency to meet transactional needs. The Fed admits this, in saying it reacts to the public's greater seasonal demand for cash needs around the holidays, for example.

That raises the question of whether the government has any way to directly affect the remaining *'non-currency'* quantity of the money supply.[9] As we have seen, the public itself creates any new money in the aggregate by borrowing from banks. The government does not have direct control creating or dissolving this newly loaned bank account money, as it is created by the private banks when their customers borrow from them. However, the Fed has tremendous indirect leverage in encouraging borrowing, and thus money supply growth, by lowering interest rates. However, as the Fed cannot drive interest rates any lower than zero, there is a limit to how much money the Fed can encourage the public to borrow this way.

Another way the Fed can grow the money supply is to simply buy debts in the open market. Typically, the Fed buys US Treasury debts. If a private institution or individual sells Treasury securities to the Fed, the Fed in return sends a credit to their bank balance, thus increasing the money supply by buying the debt. The Fed can send existing money from its account or simply create new dollars. Schiff's worry is that if the market for Treasury debt becomes im-

---

9 The non-currency portion of the "M2" money supply, commonly used for transactions, includes checking, savings and money market accounts and certificates of deposit below $100,000.

balanced with all sellers and no buyers, only the Fed will remain as a buyer. If this happens it is true that there may be little choice but to create money to pay off Treasuries as they mature (see Chapter Eight).

My first point in this chapter was that the usual economists' take on money supply inflation is to simply presume it. They assume it is simple, like the circuit voltage. "More money chasing the same amount of goods causes inflation" gets retold so many times that most economists don't even question it. It is a cornerstone assumption of Schiff's doom scenario. The problem is, as reasonable as it sounds, it simply isn't true.

There are cases where it was true, such as the gold fields of mid-19th century California.[10] But there are many other cases where a correlation doesn't even exist, or the inflation was much smaller than the money supply increase would predict.

In the California gold fields, you clearly had a case where *everybody knew* the money supply was increasingly rapidly. Money was gold, and money supply creation was in fact the main industry the great majority of the population was engaged in – pulling gold out of the ground. Secondly, the gold was easier and cheaper to get. When the miners had lived back East, it might require a month's work to earn an ounce of gold. In the gold fields, they might find an ounce in a day. So money was clearly known by all to be *much more abundant*, and *cheaper* in terms of effort, to

---

10   The gold money supply increased rapidly, clearly causing rapidly escalating prices.

obtain. At the same time, establishment of supply lines to California took a while to catch up after the Gold Rush, so supplies were quite scarce at first, and their prices soared in terms of gold. *Greater abundance that was obvious to all and greater ease in obtaining gold (money), along with scarce supplies clearly explain why money-supply price inflation happened in that economy.*

Backwards reasoning from hyperinflated disaster economies supposedly proves a connection between printing currency and inflation, but the test of a predictive theory is how well it predicts, not how well it back-tests in a few cherry-picked examples in hindsight. In other words, if you look at Zimbabwe or Weimar Republic's hyperinflation and knowing that those countries created a most extreme exponential increase of their money supplies (while having other very grave political, social or economic problems) it is easy to connect the dots and find causation from hyper-printing to hyperinflation. However, if you try to correlate less extreme, yet substantial, money supply changes to inflation rates in healthier economies, the correlation does not hold up well and money supply change does not quantitatively predict inflation. Such correlations seemed to hold true during the 1970's in the US but not during other periods.

Additionally, some economists argue that inflation causes greater demand for money by the public, so that the causation is actually the reverse – inflation leads to money supply growth. This actually makes much sense. We have seen that the money supply increases when there is increased public demand for loans from the banks. Therefore, if prices are higher, the public will be demanding larger loan amounts for just the same asset purchases in the economy. Larger loan amounts from price inflation thus would cause creation of more money.

I have also shown with the poker game example that it is theoretically possible for a large money supply inflation to happen where the economy and nobody actually gets hurt. That couldn't happen in the real world. However, if wages generally keep pace with high inflation, and if the inflation is roughly consistent for a wide variety of goods and services across the economy, the damage from double digit annual inflation could be mitigated somewhat and the economy remain viable.[11] However, there would surely be accompanying high interest rates, which put the squeeze on an economy. Then creditors holding bonds that are not inflation-adjusted would suffer terribly, while the long term debtors would get an "inflation windfall" in being able to repay with much cheaper dollars down the road.

In the poker game, the house owed a debt of $1 for every chip to be redeemed. The chips were like bearer bonds with a $1 face value. Since the bonds (chips) were adjusted at the time of inflation from a $1 face value down to 50 cents, the host did not get burned by having to repay $2000 for the 2000 $1 chips when he only had taken in $1000. With no inflation adjustment he would have lost $1000 just for being the bank.

---

11   This describes the stagflation of the 1970's.

Certain conditions are required for money supply inflation to happen. It doesn't just happen because more money is provided to an economy, like voltage. Remember that inflation equals rising prices,[12] so for money supply inflation to occur, sellers of goods (and workers, who are sellers of their labor) must be actively and mindfully raising their prices in reaction to the 'easier' supply of money. For this to happen:

1) *It must be widely observed that money is significantly more plentiful.* 'Stealth' money supply increases would not necessarily cause inflation, even if quite large. It must be part of the common experience of the price-setters in the economy that money has become more plentiful. If those who set prices don't know of any more money, they can't react to it. Frankly, I don't see how this observability can happen in today's economy. Businesses are focused only on money in regard to their own transactions, so more currency being in print or in bank balances somewhere wouldn't likely change the experience of most businesses in the least, other than in greater potential for sales. In contrast, in the fishing village everybody could not help but know when the fish run was a particularly abundant one.

2) *The new money must be 'cheaper' to obtain.* In the

---

12   In Chapter One, I defined inflation as 'generally rising prices', the common understanding of the word. Defining inflation as 'an expanded money supply' regardless of price changes, as many economists do, is very confusing for the layperson. All my references to "inflation" refer only to rising prices.

81

village example, more fish packed into the narrow riverbed means it is faster to fill one's basket. In this case since villagers can wade and simply grab the struggling fish in mere inches of water, there is little effort, so no premium for effort in obtaining extra 'fish' money. There is no time lost to get more fish during the times when they are packed more closely in the stream.

On the other hand, if the river is much wider so that during very abundant salmon runs the fish are quite spread out and much more effort is required to take advantage of the abundance and fill many baskets, the extra effort will deter some from trying, and limit the catch for those who do work hard. They will be limited by what can be accomplished in the hours in a day, and pay with their extra labor. The lack of 'ease' in obtaining the abundant money will put some limit on the 'effective' money supply, and also put limits on the inflation. The fish harvest would be too 'dear' then to just give away, since it required a lot of work.

So if money is more plentiful, but there are strings attached to obtaining it, the money will not be viewed so cheaply (inflated). Thus, if the government greatly increases the money supply in the form of *loans that must be repaid*, or in the form of *jobs where work is required* (i.e. the New Deal), this is very different in the perceptions of the recipients than simply receiving government money with no strings. Hard-earned money is dear and valuable money.

Remember that banks can create legitimate money by simply waving a magic wand and having it appear in a borrower's bank balance once the loan papers are signed. The money couldn't be easier to create, yet this system has worked for hundreds of years without creating hyperinflation. Why is that? *The obligation to pay the principal and interest keep the money's value high, preventing borrowers from psychologically cheapening or debasing its value.* Also, wherever the borrower goes with this bank-created money, he sees confirmation that it is highly valued by others. Perception is value.

The fact that the banks' routine, incredibly easy creation of money does not cause rampant inflation in our economy is the strongest possible evidence to debunk the idea that massive Fed money creation to pay the government's debts must create inflation. The sellers of the retired Treasuries would then be the owners of newly created US dollars. *Since they paid dearly for the dollars with their T-bills, those dollars will not be cheapened in their minds.* The Treasury sellers may simply accept the Fed's newly printed cash as thoughtlessly as borrowers from banks accept their 'magic wand' loan proceeds. With no perception of cheapened, easily obtained money, there would be no particular reason to believe there would be money supply induced inflation.

What happens when the government does simply hand out money to everybody with no strings attached? For example, if the government were to print up extra $100 bills and send ten, or $1000, to every household in the country, this might possibly cause money supply inflation, but it should be very little. A thousand dollars multiplied by 125 million households is $125 billion. Adding $125 billion to the $7.5 trillion money supply could plausibly cause a bit of inflation, but it would be impossible to say whether it would for sure and by how much. It is not just mathematics, like a natural law. The perceptions and economic activities of millions come into play.

Most prices are set by free markets in this country and not the government. How would the millions of business managers who set prices and the general public view the extra $125 billion in money supply? *I imagine they wouldn't even think twice about it for the purpose of setting prices (or wages)!* They would just be glad for the extra $1000 bucks and be on their merry way. Isn't this exactly what happened last year? I heard no complaining that the Economic Stimulus Act of 2008 was inflationary![13]

On the other hand, suppose the US Treasury sends a check for one million dollars to every household in the country, creating an increase in the money supply of *$125*

---

13 Of course, the federal Economic Stimulus Act of 2008, sending checks of up to $600 per taxpayer and $300 per dependent, was funded through taxes or borrowing, not increasing the money supply through printing currency. However, often money-supply inflation is defined as "more money chasing the same amount of goods", so by this definition it would not matter whether the Act were funded by printing greenbacks or the 'foreign' buying of US Treasuries that has some gold bugs so worried.

trillion. Obviously this is off the charts, increasing the aggregate M2 money supply *sixteen-fold*. But what would happen to our economy if the government did this? The answer will not come from any mathematical formula. Psychology and common sense tell us pretty surely what would happen:

When people opened their mail to find a $1 million check from Uncle Sam, they would be ecstatic, having a sudden windfall of more money than many households earn in a lifetime. But then they would wonder if it were a mistake and Uncle Sam would be taking it back. They would read the accompanying letter and find out the $1 million was theirs to keep. Joy would return - *briefly*. Soon they would find out that everybody else also got million dollar checks. The media would be buzzing – it would be major breaking news like no other. Some high government officials would quickly be interviewed by the media, and say it was no hoax and that American households should enjoy the gift.

But then the joy would quickly turn negative. Everybody would wonder why the government did this and call it irresponsible. They would assume it was somehow an act of desperation for some deep, dark government problem. The cost would be mind-numbing. There would be cries of extreme government incompetence (you think it's bad now!), and fears that the government was trying to cover up a rotten financial system and prevent some kind of a collapse. There would be massive extra money suddenly in people's bank accounts and *everybody would know it.*

For this reason, surely many prices would get immediately reset to much, much higher levels because everybody knew an insane amount of money had just been created out of thin air. The money supply increase was extremely large and *costless to recipients*, so there would be a universal psychological devaluation of the dollar. It is reasonable to think such a psychological shock might ignite hyperinflation.

The irony here is that sending these large checks to everyone could in fact, in and of itself, be the sole cause of a dollar collapse, even if nothing else in the financial system or economy were problematic! The million dollar checks would shake the public's trust in our money and government to the very core.

Ultimately confidence is everything in a money system. If confidence in it is complete, it does not matter whether it is fiat or intrinsically valuable currency. The medium of exchange being virtually universally perceived as valuable and accepted is all that is needed. The gold bugs will scoff and say this is false, that one day fiat money is bound to fail. I agree that fiat money will eventually fail, simply because nothing human lasts forever. Ice Ages come and go. But the US dollar's demise could be 5,000 years away. The basic confidence of Americans that Federal Reserve Notes are in fact very valuable will be an incredibly tough nut to crack, though. We are nowhere near that.

I have also shown that gold may be intrinsically valuable to 99% of the world's population, but there are those few, like some of the Native American tribes in nineteenth century America, who did not value it. *That is enough to prove that even "intrinsic" value is completely subject to perceptions.*

Interestingly, Uncle Sam's $1 million checks could be a relative non-event if the people universally agreed to make it so. In theory, all that would be necessary would be to simultaneously adjust all prices, all wages, and all debts to a new, much higher level to reflect the added money supply, just like the poker game. Of course, in practice it would be very difficult to come up with the actual values, and people would greedily bicker to adjust the new prices, wages and debt amounts to their own relative advantage. But the issuing of the $1 million checks need not disrupt our economy a bit. After all, it's just a bunch of envelopes being mailed out. Why should that disrupt the value of the farmers growing their crops, the teachers teaching young minds, the carpenters building a home, the road crew fixing holes, the truckers hauling goods....

In this vein, there are two 'US economies' in simultaneous existence. One is the tangible, *'physical economy'* where workers get up in the morning and go to work to produce some value in the form of a good or service for a customer (or employer), and the other economy is just a representation of the physical economy in a *financial system* of prices, markets, and transfers of dollars, in exchange for value received. In most transactions, one party receives a good or service produced in the physical economy and the other party receives (unless it is barter) a financial representation of value. The physical economy of humans doing productive work, and the consequent accumulation of wealth, are ultimately the true components of the United States' public and private net worth. As innovation allows new possibilities, and worker productivity is improved, that accumulation occurs at any ever-increasing rate, and so the aggregate net worth grows in a compounding fashion over time.

The other *'financial economy'* of money, prices, and markets, is *only a reflection* of the true, physical economy. It allows us to exchange pieces of the true economy through representative securities. The financial economy's markets can affect the real, physical economy significantly, especially in the short term, but regardless of financial market volatility, the financial markets' values must ultimately be loosely tethered to the true, productive economy in the long run. Benjamin Graham said it best when he said that in the short term the (stock) market is a voting machine, but in the long term it is a weighing machine. No analogy could ring truer. Thus, if 35 years from now GDP is at three times its current level, the stock market will necessarily have had to 'tag along' higher for the most part. The stock market may have only doubled if it's being very pessimistic, or may have quadrupled in a booming bull, but the underlying economic reality will have pulled it up - along with GDP. This principle is why the Dow Jones Industrial Average (DJIA) loosely paced national economic growth and corporate profit growth as it rose a spectacular *175-fold* over the course of the 20th century.

Another way to look at the duality of simultaneous physical and financial economies is the myth of 'wealth evaporation' in the financial markets. When the housing and stock markets tanked in 2008, the media and pundits howled over the mass 'evaporation of wealth' that had occurred. Actually, wealth does not 'evaporate' from fallen market prices. It should be taken as a figurative, not literal, expression. Of course it is painful when one's portfolio declines, and a reminder that there is no guarantee of positive returns, but what is forgotten is that a share of stock is actually a piece of the ownership in a business. That is what a shareholder truly owns, and that ownership never 'evaporates' (bankruptcy notwithstanding). *The current share price is only a report of the most recent sale – nothing more.* When share price falls dramatically, the ownership interest has not evaporated in the least. The same portion of the company is still owned.

Owners of businesses recognize that at some points in the business cycle the markets are too optimistic and share prices get carried away, while at other times they are too pessimistic and prices get carried away the other direction. If you can be sure the business behind the shares you own has a sound and profitable future, you can sleep easy when the market price of the shares declines, or even buy more shares. *A good business is unchanged by its stock price changes.* This illustrates how the two simultaneous economies coexist, with the physical economy (business) being the one that prevails over the financial economy (share price) in the long run.

We must not forget the underlying physical US economy when we think of the possibility of hyperinflation. Hyperinflation has historically occurred in deeply ravaged economies of their own right, before any government printing spree. Our currently depressed economy would have a long way to go to worsen to that degree. The nation's physical economy's assets and production are sound in aggregate, even after debt is subtracted. We think a housing bubble, large and questionable debt overhang, current 7% unemployment, a bit of deflation and losing a couple points of GDP are bad, but those problems don't compare at all to economies that have suffered hyperinflation.

The Weimar Republic (Germany) was completely buried in many years of heavy debt payments for all the damage it caused by World War I, so its net worth was well below zero:

> "The total reparations demanded was 132,000,000,000 (132 billion) gold marks which was far more than the total German gold or foreign exchange."[14]

In effect, the Weimar government was bankrupt so there was little to lose for the government by printing away the debt. Europe had just experienced a physically devastating

---

14   "Inflation in the Weimar Republic", Wikipedia.org.

World War, so adding a completely failed currency to the list of things to rebuild may have seemed like more solution than problem. Hyperinflation was just one piece of the larger mass chaos of World War. Weimar's hyperinflation also had the silver lining of unshackling Weimar from the insurmountable war debt.

The US government, on the other hand, has a colossal amount of net worth (once you've subtracted the national debt from all the land, natural resources, and military and other assets that it owns, not to mention its tax claims on all future US economic activity and its reputation as the world leader as an asset). Therefore it is not in the government's interest to hyperinflate away the national debt as Weimar did. Without such incentive, and considering the world-changing upheaval destroying the US dollar would bring, it is safe to say that our political leaders, the Federal Reserve, and the foreign holders of our currency and national debt at least will not *want* US dollar hyperinflation, and will seek to avoid it. Such was not necessarily the case in the Weimar Republic.

CHAPTER SIX

Other Inflation:

Producer Costs and Creeping Inflation

COST PUSH INFLATION

A more accurate predictor of inflation than money supply growth, of many consumer goods at least, is input price changes. This is commonly called *cost-push inflation*, which is roughly measured in aggregate by the Producer Price Index, or PPI. Since our economy is based largely on petroleum, oil price swings can quickly get factored into prices of products from apples to toilet paper. Anything with transportation cost being a significant percentage can be affected when diesel fuel jumps from $2 to $4 per gallon as it did. In addition to oil prices affecting us through transportation costs, they affect us because petroleum is often a direct ingredient in a variety of products, such as anything made of plastic. It is also used in myriad chemical processes to manufacture modern materials of all kinds. I won't dwell on the point, but I think it is easy to see that if oil prices rise, the manufacturing, material, and transportation cost combination can get passed on to the consumer very quickly as general inflation across the economy.

Cost-push inflation is the most objective type of inflation to observers. If the price of beef is well known to be skyrocketing due to cattle disease, people will be understanding when they see the results at their grocers. The hard times may also be fairly limited to affected industries.

Schiff predicted that by now commodities of all kinds including oil and precious metals would be soaring (his predictions are not always right, as commodities are down sharply across the board). As of this writing, gasoline costs $1.60 per gallon in my town, down from as high as $4.19 just 5 months ago. The decline is unprecedented. Needless to say, the potential for this recessionary input *deflation* to offset some of the (supposedly) inflationary government policies might actually work out quite well!

The gold bugs' prediction of excessive money supply inflation from government stimulus borrowing/spending is abstract mental gymnastics; an arena where quantitative predictive models do not work. The drop in oil, though, is sure to be a great help for the pockets of consumers and businesses nationwide. I wouldn't be surprised if corporate earnings post positive surprises from the lower oil cost (and general cost cutting), and the stock market gets a lift in 2009. Oil is ubiquitous and its price effects are very real and now.

CREEPING INFLATION

Cost-push inflation can be very real and measurable when input prices rise. *Money supply* price inflation might be real at times, though in a vast and complex economy such as ours, it's likely that the amount of any price inflation caused is lower than the percentage increase of the money supply - perhaps much, much lower. But I believe the kind of inflation that we experience most commonly in our society is what I'll call *creeping inflation.*

Creeping inflation is what happens when people react to their *expectation* of inflation. (Cost-push inflation, on the other hand, is a reaction to an actual experience of a specific price inflation.)

If I am a shopkeeper and I assume my store rent, utilities, supplies, inventory or labor costs will be rising over time, I may creep up my prices each year preemptively to break even, or better. Creeping inflation is often viewed as something of a right. Oftentimes prices are set higher than expected cost increases because owners tire of their business and require ever greater profit to keep doing the same old grind. Also, as workers gain years of experience they tend to believe they are worth more, and expect yearly increases, even after inflation. Often they are no more valuable but they still feel entitled to more pay. Years ago our government began tying its workers' salaries and pensions to the Consumer Price Index (CPI). This saddles a creeping inflation onto the whole economy in the form of a growing government budget just to fund the same agencies and programs at the same level.

It is interesting to note that during many periods before World War II, there was little to no inflation for stretches of many years. Often the gold standard is credited for maintaining constant price levels during those times. The psychology of creeping inflation was apparently not present, possibly because most economic activity occurred within local, tight knit communities and there was less general cynicism than today.

The good news about cost-push inflation and creeping inflation is that they are seldom anything more than modest. Moderate cost-push inflation can't cause general panic. Creeping inflation also tends to be quite modest because people do not want to price themselves out of business, or appear too greedy. Money supply inflation is thus the only type with the potential to lead to hyperinflation.

CHAPTER SEVEN

Fiat Currency, Backing, and Faith

As far as the fiat nature of our paper money, I completely understand and agree with the gold bugs that it is *intrinsically worthless*, but I firmly believe it is extremely unlikely that fact will ever have any bearing on Americans' confidence in it, unless hyperinflation were to actually occur first. For almost half a century, intrinsic worthlessness has not created any general loss of confidence in the Federal Reserve Note. It would take a drastic and universal psychological sea change, and visibly obvious, drastic impoverishment of the American economy and way of life, to begin to erode our confidence in our daily greenbacks and create a hyperinflationary spiral. The value of our currency is far too ingrained psychologically and we have not been challenged by war on our own soil, revolution, or massive civil unrest. Our economy and nation simply do not resemble those of Zimbabwe or the Weimar Republic in actual strength and productivity, or in the minds of people.

A ubiquitous phrase heard from the media following the terrorist attacks of September 11, 2001 was "our way of life will never be the same". How untrue! On the home front, the only (and quite minor) disruption to a typical American's way of life has been increased airport security. Compare this to a truly disrupted society such as that experienced by the people of Iraq since 2003, for example: the bombing of many buildings, bridges, and roads; the Iraqi army obliterated; friends and relatives killed; regime change; a slow rebuilding process; electricity and water utilities not working for months or years; shortages; collateral damage; ineffective police; influx of terrorists and continued bombings; foreign military occupation; and a new democratic government, all in a short time.

In the past, hyperinflation has tended to occur in places of much greater physical disruption – war on the nation's own soil, revolution, famine, epidemic, fascist rule, and the like. The US financial crisis, recession and current stock market deflation seem frightening to us, but barely register on the fright scale compared to what the citizens of Iraq, Zimbabwe or Weimar experienced. We have had zero physical disruption – only financial disruption. Even the financial disruption has not been truly extreme – an over 30% drop in the stock market is something the US has experienced every couple of decades, on average. Home prices are down a lot, but at a reasonable level. Homeowners are not wiped out of equity if they bought at the reasonable prices of the past. Some commodity prices have been very volatile, but there have been no shortages of any kind, so many Americans' daily life is unchanged due to the financial crisis and recession. The most significant change is probably the loss of jobs and income for the unfortunate. The decreased gasoline usage when it's price was $4.00, and other household cost cutting has been a secondary difference in daily life.

I have shown in Chapter Two that psychology and perceptions are at the very heart of all value, even in the case of gold. I think even gold bugs would agree that we won't need to worry about a total loss of faith in the dollar unless massive inflation occurs first. It would make no sense to say that if hyperinflation were caused by a combination of flooded money supply and widespread loss of faith in the money, that the hyperinflation could possibly happen *before* there was a serious loss of faith.

In other words, Americans would have a good degree of faith in the greenback *"as long as it worked"*. If you could still spend it and it was universally accepted, with any inflationary loss of purchasing power being only moderate, that's all it would take to have faith, even if the printing presses were going full speed. If for some reason all prices were rising completely wildly in very short time spans, then *that* would destroy the faith.

An indicator that the public losing faith in Federal Reserve Notes is unlikely comes from contemporary stories during this financial crisis. There have been reports of currency stashes both lost and found. In a local Whole Foods store recently, a shopper found several thousand dollars in a cereal box that had been returned by a forgetful elderly woman. Another local thrift store shopper found several thousand dollars in a pair of boots from an estate. These instances demonstrate that the financial crisis has some people fearful of holding money in banks, but not in US paper money that is intrinsically worthless. This widely held belief that our currency is a safe stash would have to change for hyperinflation to sweep the country.

Of course a government hard-asset currency backing, such as the gold standard, would serve to anchor the currency faith much more solidly in times of panic and crisis, and likely cause some monetary discipline in government. *However, government monetary discipline is far from guaranteed by any gold standard.* That seems to be a common fallacy of the gold bugs. It would be very easy in crisis times for officials to print money far beyond gold reserves on the overwhelming likelihood that the public wouldn't try to redeem all the currency for gold at once. It may be equally easy for that mindset to spill over to printing excess currency in non-crisis times, too, to achieve political ends. It can be argued that some system of audits could prevent this, but I doubt a corrupt administration could not 'cook the books' to get around that. In this sense, a return to a true 'gold standard' might turn out to be illusory.

The exact same principle has always been at the heart of our banking system. It is called 'fractional reserves', and creates an ever-present potential for disaster! Yes, all banks in our economy, no matter how conservatively and ably run, would collapse immediately should large numbers of depositors demand withdrawal in currency. It makes no difference whether it is good times or bad; it could happen in a single day, and force the banks to seek shelter with the FDIC. It works like this:

When I deposit money at my bank, whether it be

in savings, checking, or a certificate of deposit, the bank does not need to keep sufficient cash on hand to cover my making a total currency withdrawal. By banking regulation, the bank is required to keep, at most, 10% of transaction deposits available for cash withdrawal at a given time.[1] Should a bank's depositors all at once demand to withdraw everything in currency, the bank would have to borrow the cash from another bank, or the Fed. Should a panic cause a widespread depositor run on the banks for currency, there is only about $1 in cash for every $10 in bank deposits (M1) in aggregate. *So the whole banking system is always in a potentially precarious position.* Should anything precipitate a panic of mass withdrawals, it is a house of cards by its very nature.[2] However, it is a worthwhile gamble for the nation as it gives savers the vehicle and incentive to allocate capital for others to generate economic growth and prosperity. Without the availability of such capital, we might still be in a horse and buggy economy.

I hope I have convinced you at this point of the intractability of psychology and perceptions to the market value of any asset, including currencies. We are a nation that has thrived like no other in history by exchanging completely worthless pieces of paper with each other for nearly half

1 Transaction deposits are (checkable) deposits that can be withdrawn at any time without penalty. There is no reserve requirement for time deposits (CD's).

2 If a mass-withdrawal panic ever happened, the government could effect emergency measures and freeze funds. There were several panics in US history that caused mass bank failures before the Federal Reserve was created in 1913. Depositors stood to lose everything in panics, as there was no federal insurance then.

a century. Almost nobody gives the worthlessness any thought. The only thing this peculiar green paper has going for it is the completely unshaken belief of the entire nation and world that it is very valuable. I firmly believe faith in the currency is the *only* necessary ingredient in its success. It's a matter of how deeply ingrained that faith is, when push comes to shove. *The faith in the currency is linked to the level of faith in the economy behind it and in the perceived strength and integrity of the issuing government.*

We are the envy of the world in so many respects, and more ingenuity, innovation, refinements of efficiency, and development of breakthrough ideas continue to have their origin within our shores than in any other place or time. Even our pop culture (Hollywood, music, athletes, and various entertainments including technological gadgetry) have dwarfed other nations, planting indelible impressions of US greatness around the world. I think these factors have helped cement in many people's minds, especially foreigners holding the majority of US debt, that the United States' economic assets are very valuable and its currency desirable. The dollar's recent sharp upward spike during the current crisis suggests it is so. That's not to say that the dollar *should* have rallied, but those who are knowledgeable and rational do not get preferred status in setting market behavior.

CHAPTER EIGHT

Mitigating Factors in the

Astronomical Government Borrowing

Schiff has characterized "the printing press" as the nail in the US dollar's coffin – the catalyst sending it on an irreversible hyperinflationary death spiral. He says that foreigners' appetite for US Treasury debt will cease and the government will have no choice but to massively print money in desperate attempt to prop up the collapsing economy and service the burgeoning debt.

This is a plausible line of reasoning. I'm not sure how likely it is, but the logic does work. Fortunately, as I discuss in Chapter Nine, most economic arguments make some kind of perfect sense, yet fail to actually predict anything. It is just the nature of macroeconomic arguments to be vastly inadequate by oversimplification.

It's probably safe to say that all Americans are deeply concerned about the astounding increase in government spending we've seen in stimulus packages and "bailouts" Congress has recently authorized. The three main questions are whether the money is being used wisely, how manageable paying off the debt will eventually be, and whether we are approaching the limit of what the US Treasury can borrow from investors, particularly investors abroad. I'll address them one by one. I don't pretend to know all the complexities and future implications – no one can – but I think it is worth pointing out that there are some genuinely hopeful and positive factors about all this debt and spending. On the other hand, there is a very serious problem with the aggregate amount of national debt, especially the large portion coming due in the next few years.

It is the nature of government spending and borrowing to seem very high during economic recessions (in Keynesian stimulus-based economics). Deficits will run even higher than the high spending would normally indicate because tax receipts are lower due to lower employment, lower consumer and capital spending, and capital losses instead of capital gains. Alternatively, during boom times, responsible government can and should use flush boom revenues to create budget surpluses and pay down some of the national debt.

As far as the first question of whether the money is being used wisely – that is a really difficult question. I don't think anybody will ever be able to say for sure. However, as I showed in Chapter Three, *economic stimulus through spending does unquestionably provide a very real benefit.* Dollars flowing from the government into the economy really do enrich businesses and create jobs, and through the dollars' continuous recycling provide rippling benefits compounded by the velocity of money. If President Obama delivers on his promise of New Deal-type infrastructure spending, the value in job creation and government dollars cycling their way through the economy will be real. (Also, the nation will benefit by a badly needed reconstruction of highways, bridges, levees and the like.) The question comes on the cost end.

Keep in mind that every time a stimulus-package dollar changes hands, the government gets a piece back in the form of tax revenues. So if the Treasury loans $25 billion to XYZ corporation (or grants XYZ a $25 billion contract to repair bridges) as the money is spent by XYZ and re-spent repeatedly down the line, the IRS gets a piece of the action from all wages, salaries, corporate and private profits generated from the loan money. The States, too, will gain in sales tax revenues from each trip the monies make in the purchases of goods eligible for sales tax collection. As long as the money stays moving (or invested) the government's accumulated tax receipts grow with each pass from one hand to the next. *This extra tax generation effectively reduces the borrowing cost for the government considerably, and might easily provide for more than the measly .2% to 3% interest that new issue Treasuries are currently paying.* It's quite a racket, really, when you can tax money whenever it moves, and then borrow at the cheapest rates on earth in 50 years, lend it out and watch it move! Then if the XYZ Corporation pays the interest and survives to pay off the loan, the government makes out very well indeed. So not all is lost in issuing more Treasury debt. Some of the dollars work their way back to the government coffers as taxes, and it's additionally reasonable to expect Uncle Sam to profit on *some* of the loans and asset security purchases.

The case of the $225 billion in preferred stock purchases of 9 major banks is similarly stacked for the government. These securities yield 5% to Uncle Sam for the first 3 years, and 9% after that. This is profitable for the Treasury as it borrows the money by issuing Treasury securities paying at most 3%.[1] As long as the banks pay the preferred shares' 5% dividend and survive to buy back the preferred stock (once it yields 9% the banks will likely want it off their backs), the taxpayers will make out quite profitably indeed. If the banks don't survive, the taxpayers have a preferred bankruptcy claim over the common stockholders and may thus have somewhat limited losses. The government has to be repaid in full before common stockholders receive a penny in bankruptcy. So there is a good chance that even in bankruptcy, the government would receive some valuable assets. Banks are highly leveraged, but the debt is counterbalanced by assets (supposedly valuable ones). These asset values have not proven to be junk yet – it is a waiting game. Mortgages, in particular, should hold up well from fire-sale levels due to the collateral. Consumer debts may be sketchy, but they won't *all* default. A good many borrowers will continue to make payments. So the government has a good chance of being made whole in a number of cases and even profiting on the bank capital infusions.

As consolation for any losses in the 'bank bailouts' preferred stock/warrants purchases, the government at least knows that the banks' cash-infusion gamble may have

---

1   Treasury long bonds currently yield under 3%, while short maturity bills only cost the government less than ½% annual percentage yield (APY) in interest.

helped stave off a widespread, panicked depositor run on the banks, which would truly have been a nightmarish scenario (see Chapter Seven).

As far as the Troubled Asset Repurchase Program (TARP), the original idea of open market buying, and thus creating price-support in the market, for mortgage-backed securities was a good one, where the taxpayers had much more profit potential than loss potential! As Warren Buffet pointed out in an interview on Charlie Rose's program, any bailout money used to purchase troubled assets is not being *spent;* it is being *invested.* In fact, Mr. Buffet offered to match 1% of the Treasury's $700 billion originally allocated for the plan with $7 billion of his own holding company's money, investing alongside the Treasury. Considering that he is probably the greatest investor today, known for his uncanny ability to *not lose money* in an investment, and his offer carries tremendous assurance. Unfortunately, the Treasury thus far, under Secretary Paulson, has backed off on purchasing any mortgages.

US Treasury purchases of debts and preferred shares also have an advantage in being assets on the government's books to offset the corresponding liabilities of their cost. So the borrowed funds the Treasury uses increase the national debt, but the assets added to the books counterbalance the corresponding debt, and could potentially be sold to raise cash in a liquidity crunch.

The reason mortgages at fire-sale prices are a good deal and relatively riskless is that a tangible asset such as a house and land has unquestionable, enduring real value. There is a floor to how far home values, and thus mortgages, can fall. In fact, there is generally no better collateral than residential real estate. A house can't be faked or absconded with by the borrower. It can be readily inspected for condition problems, so there isn't much uncertainty of what is actually owned, unlike in stocks where you must rely on the accuracy and honesty of the financial reports. Everybody needs a place to live, so there is always a market for homes, and they are among the most reliable of assets to appreciate over time. They are the first investment choice for those who begin to have disposable income to save, so the oversold home market has created bargains and can only be relatively near a bottom, with considerable latent demand to provide support from prices falling much further.

If a modest home in California was bubble-priced at $500,000, then it will start looking quite attractive below $300,000 and probably see a floor above $200,000. If the government can buy these mortgages at fire-sale market prices, the collateral couldn't be better, setting a floor to loss potential. Though there is oversupply right now of homes, with a current nationwide *annual net creation of 1 million households*, it should not be too long before the excess housing supply is sopped up at these fallen prices and home values inevitably begin ascension again.

So as far as whether the government stimulus spending and bailouts have merit, there are certainly positives and the money isn't simply being thrown away. Time will tell, and I think will vindicate the use of at least some of the emergency stimulus spending in terms of the taxpayers recouping their investment later.

The second major concern about the government's massive borrowing is whether we can afford it as a nation, and ever even pay it back. Here the news could certainly be better, but could be worse. The over $1 trillion currently proposed in deficit spending will bring the cumulative National Debt (nearly $12 trillion) to over 70% of annual GDP, which is a 50 year high. However, it is not a record. World War II spending caused the National Debt to be over 90% of the GDP in the years following the war. *Notably, this debt did not dampen the post-war economic boom*, so that by 1958 the national debt to GDP ratio was actually *down* to the 70% level of today from considerably higher. The large war debt not crippling the economy or even preventing boom times is certainly a hopeful glimmer.

Frankly, our unmanageable National Debt level is very frightening, and it continues to climb. The Treasury Department makes fairly detailed monthly reports of the Debt, but it cannot be discerned from the reports the quantities of soon maturing issues that are likely to be rolled over into new issues. *With $2.6 trillion coming due in 2009 alone, there is potential for catastrophe in this.* However, I may as well continue the spirit of optimism threading through this book and point out the positives, or potential positives, to US government borrowing.

It is critical to realize that the Treasury borrows by issuing debt that is not adjusted for inflation.[2] Consider a 30 year bond to be sold by the Treasury today, costing the government less than a meager 3% annual interest[3], that will be repaid in 2038 with dollars *not adjusted for inflation.* If inflation averages just 3% for 30 years, then the Treasury gets to pay back the principal at just 41 cents on the dollar, after inflation, keeping 59 cents in profit from inflation! Adding to that the tax revenue increases from the stimulus spending that the bonds' sale enabled, the interest cost that is below the inflation rate (negative real interest), and the fact that the government itself controls future interest rates (and to some extent influences the inflation rate) and the US government can actually *make a killing by borrowing money* in this environment! It is rather perverse and counterintuitive, but it's absolutely true. It's a sure money maker when you do the math, as long as there is inflation approaching 3% or more and these historically (50-year) low interest rates on the debt. And should inflation average much above 3%, then this long term debt practically melts away. Over a 30 year term, should GDP growth be reasonably near or above its historical average, the ability to pay off the current deficit and interest would be very secure. Remember that the government receives basically a percentage of GDP in the form of tax receipts, so that the higher the nominal GDP, the higher the tax collections.

2   Inflation-adjusted Treasury securities, or TIPS, make up only 5% of the current outstanding debt.

3   Today's 30 year Treasury bond's current yield is at a historically low 2.63% APY.

Historically average GDP growth over a period of decades would make paying off what seems like a very high deficit today to be a non-issue.[4]

For example, let's say the Treasury borrows $1 trillion to fund the current stimulus programs and budget, through 30 year bonds that pay under 3% annual interest.[5] Suppose US GDP grows on average by a conservative real (inflation adjusted) 2% per annum. In 2008, the $1 trillion borrowed is a hefty *7.7 %* of annual GDP. But that particular $1 trillion debt won't grow in the next 30 years while the nation's ability to pay (GDP) and inflation (CPI) both grow considerably. Here is the comparison when the debt comes due in 2038, *assuming just 2% annual real GDP growth*, and annual inflation rates of either 0%, 3%, or 5%:

---

4 It's critical, though, that protracted years of deflation be avoided and that the economy does grow. However, the government can try to counter any deflation somewhat with inflationary policies.

5 I use long bonds to illustrate the GDP growth and inflation effects of diminishing the debt over the long term. However, the Treasury has issued very few long bonds in recent years. Shorter maturities issued will have a far less pronounced decline in real value by maturity , as well as less decline as a percentage of GDP. However, often institutional holders routinely roll over shorter T-bills and notes upon maturity, making them effectively longer maturities for Treasury liquidity purposes, but at an even lower interest cost to the Treasury. If someone buys 5 year notes, for example, but keeps rolling them over at maturity, after 30 years the Treasury's huge windfall in the deal is even greater for only having had to pay the much lower 5 year yield for essentially a 30 year loan.

	2008	2038	2038 %GDP
Stimulus Debt:	*$1 trillion*	*$1 trillion*	-
GDP (0% inflation)	*$13 trillion*	*$23 trillion*	4%
GDP (3% infl.)	*$13 trillion*	*$56 trillion*	1.8%
GDP (5% infl.)	*$13 trillion*	*$99 trillion*	1%

Note that by the time the 30 year $1 trillion Treasury debt becomes due, it will make up only a small fraction *(1 to 4%)* of the percentage of GDP and thus can be more easily paid off. This is true with even very modest 2% GDP growth and tame inflation – lower growth than what the US economy typically experiences. With higher, more realistic growth or high inflation, or both, the $1 trillion debt could actually become, on a relative basis, trivial! With double digit inflation like the 1970's, the Treasury would make out extremely well.[6] It is easy to forget that what is a lot of money in one era is not such a big number in another. If we think back to what salaries were 30 years ago, or the price of a home or car,[7] we can project a similar quaintness to a national figure of $1 or $2 trillion thirty years hence. Then it might take $10 trillion or $50 trillion to get the public's attention.

6   The surprising quantitative analysis results of this section are completely objective. This is the one section of this book that is simply math and no opinion. One trillion dollars of deficit borrowed at today's record low Treasury yields might practically pay itself back if maturity can be postponed three decades! It depends on inflation and GDP growth over the period, and velocity of money of the current stimulus spending in bringing in additional tax revenues.

7   Actually, the 30 years from 1978 to 2008 even had relatively low average inflation.

The problem with this plan is to get the Treasury to sell, and public to buy, longer term bonds and notes, where the benefits are great for the Treasury, and maturity is postponed until GDP growth has assured the liquidity to pay. This is no doubt unrealistic at the current low yields. The buyer of long bonds pays the price – the Treasury's inflation gains will be his losses, so longer bonds may not receive nearly enough bids to sell. Shorter maturities have considerably more limited of the above mentioned benefits to the Treasury, and pose a potentially very serious refinancing problem for Uncle Sam, although the interest costs are next to nothing. It's unimaginable that a 1 year T-bill's paltry interest cost of just .4% would not be completely covered and more by the increased tax revenues generated by the spending.[8]

Of course, the $1-2 trillion of stimulus borrowing to currently avert another Depression is not all of our debt. There is *another $10.5 trillion of national debt* we have inherited from the past (thanks goes to the last eight years' administration for doubling it), making a total of around $12 trillion. However, the $10.5 trillion cannot be unspent, while today's $1-$2 trillion plus stimulus proposals are the decisions to be made now.

---

8   It is often argued that government borrowing only diverts funds that could be loaned privately more productively while still generating the same taxes for the government. This may have some truth. However, with so much of the US Treasury's debt purchased by foreigners, it is likely that some of the foreigners' alternative investments would be outside the US and not create nearly as much stimulus or tax revenues for the US. Also, during economic crises private capital needs are low as firms tend to be tightening belts rather than expanding with new capital. Only the government may be able to borrow and spend sufficiently to stimulate the economy in such times.

Considering that with stimulus borrowing/spending there is doubtlessly some stimulus benefit to the economy, some partial immediate return through increased revenues to the IRS, and some value in assets and equity received for the government's money, stimulus spending does not look as wasteful of taxpayer money as many would claim. Add to that the historically low (50 year) current borrowing cost to the government, and the great benefit received if a Depression-like deflation and debt implosion scenario is avoided, and I think the case for historic levels of government borrowing and spending right now is a good one. If it works and we avoid a Depression, the resultant benefit to GDP over the years will probably generate enough in incremental taxes to pay for the stimulus, compared to a severe recession. If it fails and we have a house of cards of bad debts, the economy will likely contract significantly and not resume much growth for some period of adjustment. *But the stimulus may still have made it much less severe than it would have been.* There is no way to know.

If we end up with a contracting, deflationary economy like the Great Depression, then I think the gold bugs have a good point in saying that the government will be tempted to try to induce inflation. I disagree that printing money or easing credit would have nearly as much inflationary effect as they say. It might cause significant inflation and might not (see Chapter Five). However, the alternative of raising interest rates much would prove politically very difficult in a recessionary environment. Either way, Schiff's idea that the government would have no choice but to print a lot of money to service the debt, since according to him it will have run out of foreigners to buy Treasuries, is somewhat speculative.

If the current deficit ends up coming to $1 trillion (the original budget had a deficit of $407 billion), the annual interest expense on $1 trillion at an average interest rate of 2% would be $20 billion. With $2.5 trillion in revenues, the $20 billion only amounts to less than a penny for every dollar coming in the IRS' door. Sure, that's still a lot of money and shouldn't be misspent, but considering the seriousness of the economic crisis, and the mitigating positive benefits of the stimulus expenditures I discussed earlier, under a penny of interest out for each dollar in seems cheap. Also, the interest on the trillion is largely fixed,[9] so years from now when inflation and GDP growth have raised the IRS' tax receipts, the $20 billion will have fallen to considerably less than a *half* a penny per revenue dollar.

My point is not to trivialize the staggering debt or make excuses for loose government spending. I only aim to point out that there is, in fact, much hope that a seemingly unpayable national debt could work out alright, and that stimulus spending does provide significant payback to the government.

As far as the third concern, running out of buyers of US Treasuries, nobody knows if and when that will happen, but it is a very serious concern. I don't want readers to

---

9   Inflation-adjusted Treasuries, or TIPS, make up only 5% of the national debt currently.

think this book suggests everything has to turn out fine. US dollar hyperinflation, in my opinion, is not a worry, but we do have a very heavy debt load that matures soon.

So far the demand for Treasuries has been very strong, and prices are in fact bid up to the highest levels in many years due to a panicked "flight to quality". *However, in addition to the estimated $1+ trillion in crisis stimulus spending to add to the 2009 deficit, as of November, 2008, the amount of the national debt coming due in the next 12 months was $2.6 trillion!! Paying off the $2.6 trillion coming due in 2009 alone is not possible.* Most of it will have to be rolled over into new debt, and I have found no government documents that address a solution to this problem.

For any investor contemplating this book for near term information or guidance, the one thing I would recommend watching the closest is how the Treasury is going to refinance the trillions in short term debt - approximately $2.6 trillion comes due in 2009 alone - plus pay for the hefty stimulus-package laden deficit. This is the gravest problem we have on the near horizon, and its resolution could be the most important factor in how the economy fares. There simply have to be buyers of huge amounts of new Treasury debt, despite paltry yields, for this to go well. *If there is any remote potential at all for hyperinflation, failure to refinance the portion of national debt coming due in the next few years will be at the heart of it.*

There is some hope in the fact that of the $10.6 trillion of national debt, over 40% is listed as "Intragovernmental

Holdings". These are such things as Treasuries held in the Social Security Trust Funds, government workers retirement accounts and pension funds, and held as 'conservative' assets on the books of a wide variety of government agencies of all stripes. Surely a large chunk of these government holdings will be plowed back into Treasuries upon maturity.

Also, many private investment funds of all kinds, such as money market funds, have stipulations to maintain portfolios with a given percentage of US Treasury securities, so they are bound (literally) to buy more as they mature. Since US Treasuries have been *historically* considered the safest interest-bearing securities money can buy, this creates a powerful inertia. As money managers are concerned with explaining their actions and keeping their jobs, to be able to say that they were in ultra-safe US Treasuries during the financial crisis is to make themselves blameless, regardless of the underlying fundamentals of US government liquidity. They're not worried – it's not their money.

Finally, with the US dollar being the world's reserve currency, there is out of necessity a colossal demand for both US currency and US interest-bearing Treasuries abroad. The Federal Reserve, in fact, estimates that more of its Notes are outside the US than within! It is reasonable to expect that much of the Treasury debt held in foreign hands will be rolled over as it matures.

The foreign US dollar demand is enhanced greatly by the mechanism of our trade deficit – when a foreign vendor receives our US dollars in payment, he has to park them somewhere, or turn around and buy US goods and services. Since the vendors aren't buying as much US stuff as they sell to us (defining the trade deficit), US dollars necessarily accumulate in foreign countries. As these dollars have accumulated, the holders have been buying US Treasuries to earn some interest in preference to none. Since the US financial crisis did not induce flight *from* Treasuries, but instead there has been a record flight *to* Treasuries, it seems safe to say that many of those demanding them simply do not see things the way Schiff says that they should. That is a big weak link in his prediction scenarios. It's the market's perceptions that ultimately count, not his. Perception of value becomes value.

So the outlook for the Treasury in 2009 and beyond to roll over the $2.6 trillion maturing debt, plus fund another approximately $1 trillion in deficit and stimulus spending, has some positive prospects. Some 40% of the national debt is held by various government agency funds, which in an emergency could be ordered to accept extended maturities. Many will purchase new Treasuries as they mature anyway. For example, the Social Security Trust Funds run surpluses, so have no need to raise cash.

Even in the private sector, many investment funds of all stripes can be counted on to maintain a stated percentage of US Treasuries in their portfolios, thus buying replacements as they mature. Additionally, many foreigners, including central banks, need to maintain holdings in the world's reserve currency. So there will be much demand for new

Treasuries in the next few years. But will it be enough? The US is still a very wealthy and strong nation by any measure. Do not buy into the fantasy that our aggregate net worth is somehow wiped out in debt. Many American families are in financial trouble but many more are not. Excessive debt will ultimately, in the long run, only be a major problem for those debtors and their creditors, and even they can eventually recover. The many Americans who live within their means will be fine in the long run.

The US government, however, has irresponsibly run up the National Debt to put the government itself in the prior group. This 'problem child' federal debt would have become manageable in time if it had been financed by long bonds. Because it was financed with short maturities, the government is at the mercy of investors to roll over these short notes, possibly repeatedly. Had we not had large deficit spending during the last eight years, we would not have had to worry about financing the needed spending now, when we are in a real crisis.

CHAPTER NINE

Do Borders Even Matter?

There has been so much written in recent years about the "global economy", where private enterprise, governments and individual investors are more globally intertwined than ever in trade relations, competition, and capital markets. New technology, changing communications and the internet have greased the wheels of global reach. It is fair to say now that capitalists, consumers and governments all have a greater eye on economic opportunities globally, and the resultant globally competitive environment will not abate. Twenty-five years ago, the idea of phoning an American business for customer service and speaking to someone in India was unthinkable. Long distance telephone rates, for one thing, made it impractical. China and many economically emerging nations have changed the landscape of the economic world in terms of both production and demand growth. Capital has more directions in which to flow more easily, and nation's businesses are increasingly financed from abroad. Global interconnectedness of economies is here to stay.

One indicator of global capital interdependency was the fact that when several US major banks and investment banks buckled beneath the weight of the subprime mortgage debacle last year, they didn't only panic the US stock market, but world markets crashed in sympathy. They typically even matched the US stock market day by day in volatility patterns. Large amounts of US securitized debt had been sold to foreign private and central banks, and no doubt additional intertwining factors made world markets highly sympathetic to the US. The global interconnectedness has never been more obvious than it is today. But what does it mean for the US?

Against this backdrop of globalism, we must reconsider the usual reflexive nationalistic impulse that tends to prevail in economic forecasts. Historically there has always been an "us" and "them" mentality between nations. Presumably, the US is a team of sorts inside our borders and the other teams are outside, and that any one team 'winning' by being very prosperous probably means its trading partners are likely somehow losing, or at least 'winning' less. Schiff describes this as the US consumers having "fooled" the Asian producers for years, and paid for their imports with debts backed by "phony wealth". *A more accurate explanation is simply that Asians exported to America because it was profitable for them, and Americans imported from Asia because the same goods were cheaper for them!* The view from the ground level of individual Asian vendors and American consumers really is that simple. As a matter of accuracy, the Asians could choose to be paid in cash dollars by the customer (or financing agent). Then both foreigners *and* Americans willingly chose to invest their dollars in the American debts.[1]

---

1 Undoubtedly two major reasons for strong foreign demand for American debts are the US dollar's status as the world's reserve currency, and the fact that foreign exporters

Though often growth or stagnation trends clearly emerge in one nation's economy compared to others, to generalize these trends to the businesses and the individuals of the nation is very often inaccurate. The bottom line is that America, and Americans, are very unlikely to experience anything approaching the wholesale, national economic destruction Schiff foresees. This is because a good many Americans, and American businesses, have valuable assets far in excess of their debt. Many will continue to have revenues beyond their expenses to grow wealth over time. In short, the current recession and debt crisis will devastate some, hurt some others to a lesser degree, and have little effect on still others.

Though the media are wont to broadcast stories of personal hardship, I personally know of many typical middle class households that are little affected by the current recession or the plunge in real estate and stock values. Their stories are too boring to be told in the media. The idea that a nation thrives together or languishes together is not a valid one in what is basically a global economy. Financial markets swooning may make it appear that a nation's fortunes are tied together, but the underlying actual economy, not the markets, drive prosperity in the long run (see Chapter Five).

---

to the US necessarily accumulate dollars, which they then seek to invest - in US dollar denominated assets. (Alternatively, they could swap for non-US currency. However, the new recipient of the dollars in a currency swap would then need to seek a parking place for them in US dollar investments.) Either way, US dollars flowing abroad from the trade deficit ultimately must seek out US dollar-based assets of some kind, or simply be held as dollars.

Keep in mind that foreign vendors to the US must pay taxes to Uncle Sam the same as if they were US citizens, so borders don't matter as much as you might think in trade. Currency exchange rates, tariffs and trade agreements can matter a lot, but the basic fact that goods are made abroad and then shipped and sold here is *not* a problem for US prosperity, other than the domestic loss of manufacturing jobs.[2]

When Schiff says foreigners will become disenchanted with US dollars, driving the dollar's value down in mass selling, there's absolutely nothing they can do to get rid of them (in the aggregate) but to dump them back in the US. Whatever they swap with other foreigners doesn't affect us, but say that no foreigner wants them so they have to spend them in the US to get some value before they drop even further. *If the dollar just experienced a sharp drop in value, when they dump them back in the US, the dollars will likely buy less while bolstering US exports and profits.* This self-corrects the trade deficit and supports the US economy, while paying back the debts on the cheap in terms of non-dollar denominated assets. The dollar's drop will be the foreigner dollar holder's loss and the US' gain.

For example, a New Zealander holding US Treasuries who wants out of a panicked US market will sell his Treasuries

---

2   Arguably, automation, robotics and computerization have "stolen" as many or more manufacturing jobs as cheap foreign labor has. This is essentially just a continuation of a long line of labor saving improvements going back centuries to such things as utilizing draft animals, harnessing steam, and the cotton gin. It is critical for American workers to seek education and skills that make them indispensable in the ever changing job landscape, just as it always has been.

into a depressed market for a loss, receiving the proceeds in US dollars. As he wants to hold no dollar-denominated assets, he will trade them for US hard goods or US-held investments denominated in a currency *other* than the dollar. Suppose he chooses to buy a New Zealand company's stock from a US shareholder with his US dollars. The US dollar, having fallen against the New Zealand dollar, will buy fewer New Zealand dollars and thus fewer stock shares. Therefore the gain for the US seller of the New Zealand company shares is greater – he gets more dollars for his shares. If I may quote myself from Chapter Four, "*When any currency gets killed against others, holders of the currency who hope to convert some portion of it into another currency pay a big price. Holders of the fallen currency who will only be exchanging the currency for assets denominated in that currency are not directly affected.*" Additionally, a US seller of foreign assets for dollars who receives more dollars during a panicked exodus, may experience high sales volumes, and high profits from the currency exchange rates of their holdings.[3]

Schiff says this massive repatriation of US dollars will cause major inflation. He has said that the huge Treasury debt, which is largely owned by foreign nations, is basically massive, latent, money-supply inflation that has been temporarily sequestered in these debts. This is nonsense, as I showed in Chapter Five. True, massive unwinding of

---

3   Of course, if the dollar falls even further, the new dollar holdings will suffer if later converting to other currency. Those only spent in the US are not directly affected by the further fall.

dollars by foreign central banks should drive the US dollar down against other currencies, from market action of a huge position being sold. That does *not* necessarily translate to correspondingly higher prices of US goods domestically, i.e. inflation. A viewpoint of a US business would illustrate:

Suppose China decides to unload a majority of its US Treasury debt and get out of the dollar. It will sell what Treasuries the market can absorb in a given time, and likely receive much of the cash in US dollars. Since it doesn't want to hold dollars, it will look at what US assets can be purchased with them. It could buy US stocks, real estate, products, or hard assets like commodities. It can also swap them in the currency markets for other currencies. However, it's large unwinding is likely to have pushed the dollar down against other currencies and make US dollar-denominated asset purchases a more attractive option than swapping their dollars for another currency at a poor exchange rate.

There is a company (that I'm sure Schiff would love!) in my state that manufactures huge mining machines that are 3 stories tall. Such mammoth machines are only manufactured in the US (even though we are just a 'service economy'), and with China's burgeoning resource needs, let's say swapping dollars for these machines looks quite appealing.

So P & H Mining gets inquiries from the Chinese government for a very large order. Now, is P & H Mining going to think "*Oh, no the Chinese have unloaded massive US Treasury debt and dollars which will cause a lot of inflation.*

We'd better jack up our prices to match this inflation."

Of course not! The huge Chinese order will be a boon for P & H Mining. If anything, it will *lower* its price on this order due to efficiencies of larger orders and to secure the large contract. *Similarly, wherever the Chinese government goes with its wad of US dollars to spend in the US, they won't creation inflation and devastation. They will create sales and profits.* Nothing could be more common sense. *The myth of many economists that more money chasing the same amount of goods must create inflation does not apply in our vast economy where the money supply is invisible to the actors, and the new money is in no way cheaply obtained. Inflation is simply a mindful raising of prices in response to perceptions – that's all. If price-setters do not perceive more abundant, cheaper money, they cannot react to what they do not see, as I show in Chapter Five.*

Therefore, the colossal amount of dollars and dollar denominated securities in foreign hands represent *latent demand* for US goods, services and assets, *not latent destructive, massive inflation.* Now, since the figure is in the trillions, I am certainly not going to say that if a huge amount of US dollars come back to the US in a short time there *couldn't be any* inflationary effect.[4] *What I am saying is that inflation is caused by businesses increasing their prices – period.*

This chapter addresses my general notion that

---

4   Nobody can know if it would have any inflationary effect and how much. It is far too complex. It will not even be knowable from a future point looking back how much inflation is attributable to such an event.

borders need not mean much in today's global economy in terms of national prosperity. Private entities, whether businesses or people, are not as tethered to their local or national prosperity as once was the case. I believe that if many Americans have lived beyond their means or bought overpriced homes or assets, that time will prove those tragedies are largely their own. Yes, these things contribute to the recession with accompanying loss of consumer demand, job loss and all around pain, but I want to point out the obvious. The simple basics often get lost when charismatic people wax on with visions of great fear, (or in the case of promoting asset bubbles, visions of greed):

People who keep themselves earning income (employable), and live below their means will increase in wealth over time. Those who don't, won't. Businesses who stay viable (profitable), and do not overleverage, will grow their wealth (retained earnings) over time. Those who don't, won't.

These are not earth-shattering concepts – they are the basics that everybody knows. However, Peter Schiff is saying that even those with responsible finances will be devastated in his coming Armageddon. The US economy, he says, will be so bad that if you simply live here and hold your wealth in US dollars, you will be severely punished for it. He sees rampant inflation as a major factor.

I'm not buying it. I think people and businesses who are responsible in keeping themselves employable and live within their means will be alright over time, just the same as it has always been. The most mundane ideas in this book have, I think, the most profound meaning. I don't think today's large, highly diversified, developed economies completely crash and burn as a national unit, or soar wildly, raising all boats, as a unit for that matter. *Individuals and businesses are primarily the makers of their own fortunes, not their nations or their neighbors.*

That's not to say borders don't matter at all. The most prominent way they do matter, with immediate and real effect, is in currency exchange rates. Floating currencies today can be rather volatile, and obviously can have an impact on a nation's trade and economic situation, and your portfolio. I think Schiff has a very good point in diversifying one's investments to multiple currencies, and to hard assets as well.

CHAPTER TEN

The Folly of Forecasts and the Great Lumping

Any student of the economy, whether serious or avocational, quickly finds there are legion opinions professing to explain the current state of the economy, and forecasts, both near and long term. These theories all have plausible linear threads of causation. Some are educated and brilliant, while others are the "hip pocket" variety. *Yet, nearly all fail to predict anything with any kind of consistency.* Macroeconomics is a theoretical discipline that just doesn't work well explaining the real world. When it does explain something, it is in obvious and simple relationships. For example, "if interest rates go down, you can expect the number of willing borrowers to increase."

Just spending a few hours in the financial and economic blogosphere will show how many highly intelligent, articulate people have figured out the next trend – contradictory to each other. These forecasts and backward-looking explanations seldom mean very much. Not only do many contradict each other, thus proving that at least some are erroneous, but it is very easy to find false causation in hindsight. It is even easier going forward. Usually, when a forecast proves wrong, the forecaster does not retract the argument, but claims that markets have not "efficiently" validated his thesis yet, or that another factor interceded, thus changing the result. We saw Schiff do this before and during the panic as commodities have plummeted, and the US dollar and US Treasuries have rallied, all strongly opposite of his predictions. The most respected Economists in history posit causal relationships that are often at odds with each other, and the debates will never end, because there usually is no correct and simple truth.

The truth is that something as complicated as our economy and markets is truly unknowable in *any* top-down approach. Peter Lynch, one of the most successful fund managers in modern times, said that he considered ten minutes a year spent trying to predict the twists and turns of the economy to be ten minutes wasted!

Nearly all lines of thought in broad economic reasoning are bound to be inadequate because factors that are moving market values more resemble the ocean than a mountain stream. You can float a leaf in a stream and predict where it will probably end up after a given time, but predicting an exact spot for a water molecule in the ocean to end up is futile.

Human intelligence, by its nature, follows a *line* of thought. Sometimes this works great, as in solving a specific engineering problem. But where human intelligence struggles and fails to understand, is when countless millions of forces are acting that cannot be isolated, or even identified. There are then far more than a few variables to consider. This is the state of Nature.

That is why humans can build astonishing marvels of engineering and technology, but cannot cure degenerative diseases or seem to make any headway in social problems such as a struggling public education system. When building a taller skyscraper, the specific problems are relatively few and individually simple in nature to understand: structural strength, flexibility in wind, resistance to fire, etc. are precisely determinable with mathematics, and thus solvable problems, one by one. A vast economy like ours is simply far too much for anybody to understand enough to predict. The best we investors can hope for is to see when a specific area is overvalued or undervalued, compared to underlying risk.

Economists, for the most part, create *mental constructs* out of general macroeconomic observations, and then proceed to argue endlessly about cause and effect between these various constructs. Having spent years mentally juggling these ideas, they tend to believe, like the gold bugs, that they have it figured out at some point.

For example, if you picture the economy as a jigsaw puzzle, you would have numerous pieces that are labeled "interest rates", "inflation", "the money supply", "producer prices", "GDP", "government spending", "stock prices", "productivity gains", "currency exchange rates", "debt levels", "disposable income", and so on. Economists are accustomed to juxtaposing these many puzzle pieces to eventually mentally to arrive at some cause-and-effect 'truths'. In effect, they are thinking that if they can only arrange all these pieces correctly, they will solve the jigsaw puzzle. Although, there is some grain of truth to many causal relationships between these concepts, the economy is too complex and ever-changing to be adequately represented by any hypothetical jigsaw puzzle. Correlations in hindsight are often weak and contingent on known or unknown factors that may not be present in the predicted scenario. So to say that the Fed's current increased money supply creation compares to Weimar or Zimbabwe is not only extremely premature at this point, but even if ramped up to much higher levels may not result in a lot of inflation. Nobody knows.

Per my views of economic value and activity from Chapter Two, I believe that all economic variables are ultimately determined by individual transactions between parties (i.e. microeconomics), not by broad concepts acting upon each other. For example, to predict "Foreigners will stop buying US debts, causing.....", is too general and too extreme to possibly be true. They won't *all* stop completely and unilaterally, and also the predicted result is much more speculative than the predictor would care to admit. *General economic prediction is suspect because markets of countless actors virtually never act in unison in the same direction.* They will perceive differently from each other. For every sale there must be a seller and a buyer. If selling of such US debts outstrips the demand, their prices will drop and yields climb, making them more attractive – the more the yields climb, the more attractive they will be to somebody. These bonds can't *all* go bad, as many Americans in any scenario will be solvent and be making their payments, so there will be some market for their debts. When investors get burned, there can be plunging values from mass selling, but generally only to a capitulation point that has undershot some intrinsic value, so strong new demand re-forms based on greed. Supply and demand seek equilibrium. In a sold-off panic market where the securities are bound to have *any* value, the fallen market at some level stabilizes. Intrinsic value acts as a powerful spring, getting ever more compressed as the price level falls further. Falling further yet becomes increasingly difficult because greed is a powerful motivator, and potential rewards then are much higher than risks. Hyperinflation Armageddon is contingent on support levels *not* happening in the US dollar and US Treasury security markets.

I hold as a motto of sorts, *"Beware of economists bearing certainty of predictions."* Schiff is certainly one who has conviction in his theories. Therein lies the problem! Schiff's conviction is not a bit subdued by the fact that his theories require complete, earth shaking changes in perceptions just a short time from now. The human inertia of millions alone would suggest the effects would be at least mitigated, even if the fundamentals were all in Schiff's court.

Schiff's conviction is also not humbled by the fact that some of his predictions have turned out the opposite, thus far. In the panic of '08, we saw US stocks and real estate fall as he predicted, but commodities, the US dollar, and US Treasuries have performed strongly in the opposite of how he predicted they would react to the crisis. Schiff devotees should heed this. Whether he is right or wrong on fundamentals, the markets obviously do not currently see it his way, even in panic, and perceptions are indeed value. Given this, why would the markets have to see it his way a couple of years down the road?

Warren Buffet speaks of the importance of investors confining themselves to their "circle of competence", however small, and *sticking to the few things that are in fact "knowable"*. He also says he has no idea whatsoever which direction the stock market will take. This humility is stunning from the single person who, by far, has had the greatest success of anybody alive in taking advantage of the stock market! Maybe Schiff's reason for being so certain about everything that will happen is that he doesn't have enough gray hair. Once an economist has all white hair, what they say may be worth a listen because they will have had a lifetime of being humbled. You will find their predictions to be in probabilities rather than certainties.

Schiff has gained notoriety for rightly foreseeing the real estate bubble prices and debt troubles that had been mounting beneath the rosy veneer of our economy. It was an excellent call, and no doubt difficult to think and speak independently a view that flew in the face of his peers. But debt is a pretty clear cut thing to see if you are looking. There is a joke in financial statement analysis that, "well, you know the liabilities are good." But sales, profits, costs, asset values and competition are often extremely tricky to project, even in the short run. When you are not talking about predicting them for one company, or even an industry, but a whole vast economy like the United States, you might as well forget it. By predicting US economic collapse, Schiff is in effect saying that due to major debt problems there will be a chain reaction that causes demand for our "service economy" GDP to fall off a cliff. He has portrayed the service economy as "flipping burgers". Does not the demise of fast food in America sound far-fetched?

Probably the most systemic problem with Schiff's predictions of the chain of events leading to his sure hyperinflation is that he has generalized to a maximal degree. He has freely used the word "all" in his appearances describing links in his chain of events, which was a problem for me from the beginning. Here again is my "nutshell" understanding of Schiff's chain of events causing hyperinflation:

1) US "phony" real estate and stock wealth evaporates; inflated consumption-based GDP is exposed by fallen demand

2) US is a bankrupt nation - (business, personal and public debts exceed assets?)

3) US Government borrows massively to stimulate economy

4) US debts default (public and private)

5) Foreigners refuse to lend anymore to US

6) Without credit available, government forced to print money in extreme amounts to fund spending and pay off maturing debt, causing hyperinflation

For the above points, ask yourself if the word "all" (or "any") reasonably applies. Is even "most" reasonable? Then ask if the supposed result requires for "all" or "most" to be inserted. I cannot imagine for the six points that such things could happen in virtual totality, as hyperinflation would seem to require.

To my way of thinking, this is a chief mistake of economists, what I call "The Great Lumping". They find a logical causal thread and then lump huge numbers of people together in seeing it that way and acting homogenously in markets. In Schiff's scenario they would need to virtually all sell with little regard to price levels (no self-correcting demand during plunges).

Consider what we know of the stock market's decline. Obviously, the Dow Jones Industrial Average (DJIA) was not about to fall from its peak of 14,000 to say, less than 100, in a few days' time. Believe it or not, this is essentially what Schiff predicts at some point for the US dollar. Hyperinflation, once it has started, is very, very fast. Currency value declines so fast in hyperinflation that people don't even want to hold it overnight! Virtually the entire population of potential buyers of US dollars (and dollar denominated assets of all kinds) would have to conclude with great conviction that the US dollar is completely worthless. We are talking about many millions of players! That is one reason why it is so extremely unlikely.

Now if hyperinflation happened *first* to the US dollar, it's reasonable to expect no foreign demand for dollars or dollar-based financial assets, but to Schiff the foreign dollar dumping is a causal link in the chain of dollar hyperinflation, so it could not happen before the hyperinflation. You can't claim that the effect of something was the cause of it.

In summary, to illustrate the folly of overly strong predictions from economic forecasts and indicators, including the stock market as an indicator, here is a favorite excerpt quoted from then Fidelity fund manager Peter Lynch:

"There was a 16-month recession between July, 1981 and November, 1982. Actually this was the scariest time in my memory. Sensible professionals wondered if they should take up hunting and fishing, because soon we'd all be living in the woods, gathering acorns. This was a period when we had 14% unemployment, 15% inflation, and a 20% prime rate, but I never got a phone call saying any of that was going to happen, either. After the fact, a lot of people stood up to announce that they'd been expecting it, but nobody mentioned it to me before the fact. Then at the moment of greatest pessimism, when eight out of ten investors would have sworn we were heading into the 1930's, the stock market rebounded with a vengeance, and suddenly all was right with the world."[1]

---

1   Peter Lynch with John Rothchild, <u>One Up on Wall Street</u>, (New York, Penguin, 1990), 75.

Afterword

My Personal Views

I have written this book as a thoughtful and objective, I believe, examination of a prediction of impending destruction of the US dollar (hyperinflation). My original purpose in investigating this topic was only to determine that view's validity for the positioning of my own investment portfolio. A drastic fall in the US dollar could certainly wreak havoc on the US economy. Since Mr. Schiff was spot-on with predicting the housing price crash and subprime mortgage crisis, and unlike many economists whose heads are in the clouds, knew the intimate details driving the subprime lending debacle, his predictions were something I had to investigate.

In the preceding chapters, I have sought to avoid expressing my personal views excessively. I do not usually care to read others' rants, and expect others also would prefer to read an analysis that is calm and objective. However, I imagine some readers may wish to know my thoughts on the US economy going forward, so I will provide them.

If I believe that Schiff is quite wrong and hyperinflation is far from certain, there is the question of what probability I would give it. In short, if the Treasury cannot refinance the large portion of the national debt coming due in the next 2-3 years, I think the possibility of a free fall, to some degree, in the dollar is real. The sudden realization of Americans that their government cannot pay its debt could be enough of a psychological shock to shake the faith in the greenback and perhaps send domestic prices significantly higher. However, if these maturing T-bills and notes are mostly rolled over by the holders, I think that hyperinflation is surely averted. Since 40% of the national debt is held by the government itself, there is much hope. Overall, I think the probability percentage of actual "hyperinflation" developing is low single digits at the most. If it happens it will be a psychological phenomenon, just as the force that makes Federal Reserve Notes valuable is purely psychological.[1] I fall in the camp that believes that most economic change is truly unpredictable, especially in valuations and in markets; the shorter the term, the more unpredictable. Examples are legion. Just think of the recent skyrocketing oil price to $140 bbl, followed by its stunning fall. It's quite unbelievable what happened in such a short time, and you can bet that most of the experts who forecast energy prices for a living are equally surprised. The quick 25% rise in the US dollar against foreign currencies as the US banks financial crisis came to a head is another shocker. Why huge numbers of investors would seek US Treasuries, yielding negative returns after inflation, at a time when the

---

1   If you really think about it, psychology is integral to the values people assign to *every-thing*. Determination of value by its nature must be a judgment of the mind.

US is doing staggering amounts of borrowing and spending is hard to understand. Why do lemmings do what they do? Yet people (or institutions) have flocked to US Treasuries in this recession, bidding up prices. If the short maturities go a little higher, people will be paying to loan the government money, rather than the other way around!

Needless to say, there is much widespread foolish behavior in the markets. It is not just from amateurs as many highly placed professionals have no idea what they are doing. I'd like to illustrate with one of my favorite quotes, from Warren Buffet again. Here he is discussing the pension fund rates of return assumptions (around 7%) from the annual reports of 4 of the 30 large Dow Jones Industrial Average (DJIA) companies in 1982:

> "...now you could buy long-term governments at 10.4%. You could in fact have locked in that yield for decades by buying so-called strips that guaranteed you a 10.4% reinvestment rate. In effect, your idiot nephew could have managed the funds and achieved returns far higher than the investment assumptions the corporations were using."[2]

It is important to note that these pension fund managers had it in their own personal interests to show the higher return of 10.4% in their reports! Since it would have been in ultra-safe US Treasuries, there was no reason not to shift

---

2   Warren Buffet; Carol Loomis, "On the Stock Market.....", Fortune, December 10, 2001

the portfolio into Treasuries, have excellent, safe returns, and send the resulting decreased pension fund charges to the bottom line, pleasing shareholders and bosses alike. It would have been win-win with no downside.

But back to my claim of unpredictability, I expect it sounds like I am copping out. How could I study economics enough to write a book about it and not have any market opinions or predictions? Well, it's just that I think *nobody benefits by guessing at the next coin toss.* If the coin turns up heads and I am right, I look good but it is meaningless, and tails, me being wrong, would also be meaningless.

My belief is that it's wise to quiet the noise of short term predictions, and follow the sage advice of Ben Graham, that the market, short term, is a voting machine, and long term is a weighing machine. We cannot predict market turns, but we can find businesses that have proven themselves to be consistent winners, and wait to purchase them only when a fallen share price provides a margin of safety and a superior return. Such fallen share prices are in rare plentitude now. Warren Buffet is on board with his October 2008, "Buy American: I Am" op-ed article in the New York Times. The article is easy to find online.

I see little reason for America's "physical economy" of workers going to work and producing the value they do, to be fundamentally changed by the fallen "financial economy" of the markets, and the debt crisis. Though debts, public and private, are at record levels, with default levels yet to be determined, the most injured will be the holders of the debts. Secondarily, these problems will affect the whole economy in terms of demand, employment levels, and so forth. I don't know how bad it will get, but the US will recover and thrive again, as we always have. Recession and contraction from overly extended credit are nothing new. We've lived through quite a few financial crises in the 232 years of being a nation and seemed to have thrived anyway, somehow.

So though I don't have any strong opinion of whether the recession will be relatively mild or will become another Depression, I do know that during *all* prior US downturns (for which stock market index records exist, since 1886), a similar fall of the Dow Jones average from its peak would prove to be an outstanding buying opportunity from the vantage point of ten or fifteen years later. Such returns have been excellent every time. There are no guarantees that this time cannot be different, but I'm much more comfortable buying a stock index fund at today's Dow average of 7,000 than last year's level of over 13,000. It just makes sense, but gauging by net fund inflows and outflows, most people were comfortable buying high and very uncomfortable about buying low!

Schiff is correct that we do have some differences this time around. The "service sector" being a greater percentage of the economy is different this time and doubtful mortgages and debt levels are very high. The US Treasury's debt level is shameful and had it been financed with long term bonds I could probably sleep a bit better.

Whether the debts of the insolvent consumers can wreak enough general havoc to cause the level of destruction Schiff believes is truly unknown. He, in fact, indirectly admits he doesn't know. He states that his dire scenario is coming in the most certain terms, but then occasionally says he hopes he is wrong.

If the past is any guide, bad debts will not devastate the whole economy for a long period of many years. The sun will start to peek through the clouds before you know it. The United States has seen much harder times than these! If the Civil War was the most tumultuous event in US history, the lesson it teaches would be that hyperinflation only happened to the *Confederacy's* currency - as evidence mounted that it was losing the war. The fiat United States currency at the time did not suffer such debasement.[3]

The most frightening current problem to me is whether the bond market is willing to refinance a huge amount of soon-maturing Treasury issues, even though they are currently a poor investment at all maturity lengths. The government's ability to borrow could be limited for the first time, and in a rational world it probably should.[4] A staggering $2.6 trillion comes due in 2009 alone, and trillions more come due in the next few years after that. If

---

3   Precious metal backing of the Union's paper money was suspended during the Civil War, making it a fiat currency. Much private and fractional scrip, and even postage stamps were used to fill the daily needs as coins had been hoarded by the public in fear.

4   Perhaps at high enough yields, trillions in new Treasuries could be sold. The resulting sudden, large, upward shock to interest rates from record low levels would be extremely unusual.

the short term debt cannot be refinanced there won't be adequate revenues to retire it and also run the government. Something drastic would have to be done. We must hope that much of what is currently invested in the short-maturing issues will not be cashed out, but instead rolled over into new issues.

The US truly is an economic powerhouse still. Previously, I have shown that our "consumption" economy really is productive. GDP is not a measure of wealth destroyed rather than created, as Schiff has said.[5] *Perceptions of value and actual demand for that value are what drive profits and jobs, creating wealth.* It doesn't matter what is being demanded or produced. It does not matter if the goods or services are sold to your neighbor or to a foreigner as exports. Wealth arises from the profits, not the nature of what is produced or sold, since the goods are gone from the producer anyway. Anybody who owns a business knows this piece of common sense, and is not fooled by other lofty-sounding ideas. And to the buyer, a durable good may be a greater asset than a fleeting service "consumed", and therefore a component of wealth, but most assets wholly depreciate over time. At the end of its useful life, a durable, manufactured good has lost its value, rendering its 'production' no different from 'consumption'.

I agree with Schiff that *if* demand for US products and services across the board falls off a cliff, we could be

---

5   Peter Schiff with John Downes, Crash Proof: How to Profit from the Coming Economic Collapse (New Jersey: Wiley & Sons, Inc., 2007), 2.

quite devastated. Well, sure, but there's no good reason to think that will happen. That is a huge "if". Real estate and stock wealth can only drop so far. Only so much debt can go bad. Consumers can only pull back spending so much. Many Americans and US businesses do have sound finances and secure jobs.

I do not believe in the persistent myth that money supply growth somehow automatically triggers inflation. People and perceptions are involved in price inflation. Demand can and does recede in recessions, but our "service sector" economy won't just fall apart, as the many Americans who do have wealth to spend, and those who do stay employed, will continue buying things, including cappuccinos!

Richard Moheban earned a BBA in Finance, Investment and Banking from the University of Wisconsin at Madison in 1987. Since then he has been an active private investor and avid student of economic news and history. He holds the belief that most macroeconomic theories are inadequate, lacking any predictive abilities due to overgeneralization. He views an examination of changing economic variables from the 'street level' view of transacting parties to be the more valuable and accurate test of economic ideas.

This book is an experiment in a slightly larger than usual font size, sans serif, for ease of reading of a difficult and text-intensive subject matter. We would love to hear your feedback on the font—and the book—at the author's website at www.hyperinflation-us.com. The author may be contacted by email via webmaster@hyperinflation-us.com.

Order Form

	Qty	Price	Total
Debunking the Hyperinflation of Peter Schiff and the Gold Bugs	____	x $17.95	____

Wisconsin residents add 5.6% sales tax ($1.01 per copy) _____

Shipping and handling to all US addresses, per order $2.00

SHIPPING TO CANADA ADDITIONAL $2.00 (US) PER ORDER;

INTERNATIONAL SHIPPING - EMAIL FOR QUOTE _____

Total enclosed $ _____

Cut out form, photocopy or simply send a note with your order

Name _____

Address _____

_____

City/State/Zip _____

Country _____

Email or phone _____

We will never rent or sell customer info

Send check or money order to:

Torn Jeans Books
3174 N. Booth St. #A
Milwaukee, WI 53212

tornjeansbooks@gmail.com